MAKE YOUR OWN OWN GREAT VESTS

To the memory of Jean Parks Hill, a unique design.

■ ■ ■ ■ ■

Editor: Leslie Dierks
Art Director: Dana Irwin
Photography: Richard Babb
Illustrations: Kay Holmes Stafford
Production: Elaine Thompson, Dana Irwin

Library of Congress Cataloging-in-Publication Data

Parks, Carol, 1942–
  Make your own great vests : 90 ways to jazz up your wardrobe /
Carol Parks
      p.   cm.
    "A Sterling/Lark Book."
    Includes index.
    ISBN 0-8069-0972-2
    1. Vests. I. Title.
  TT615.P37   1995
  646.4'5--dc20   94-35537
                                                    CIP

10 9 8 7 6 5 4 3 2 1

A Sterling/Lark Book

Published in 1995 by Sterling Publishing Co., Inc.
      387 Park Ave. S., New York, NY 10016

Created and produced by Altamont Press, Inc.
      50 College St., Asheville, NC 28801

© 1995, Carol Parks

Distributed in Canada by Sterling Publishing,
c/o Canadian Manda Group, One Atlantic Avenue, Suite 105,
      Toronto, Ontario, Canada M6K 3E7

Distributed in the United Kingdom by Cassell PLC, Villiers House,
      41/47 Strand, London WC2N 5JE, England

Distributed in Australia by Capricorn Link (Australia) Pty Ltd.
      P.O. Box 6651, Baulkham Hills, Business Centre, NSW 2153, Australia

The projects in this book are the original creations of the contributing designers, who retain the copyrights to their individual designs. The projects may be reproduced by individuals for personal pleasure; reproduction on a larger scale with the intent of personal profit is prohibited.

Every effort has been made to ensure that all information in this book is accurate. However, due to differing conditions, tools, and individual skills, the publisher cannot be responsible for any injuries, losses, or other damages that may result from the use of the information in this book.

Printed in Hong Kong.

ISBN 0-8069-0972-2

MAKE YOUR OWN GREAT

Vests

90
Ways to Jazz Up Your Wardrobe

CAROL PARKS

A Sterling/Lark Book
Sterling Publishing Co., Inc. New York

c o n t e n t s

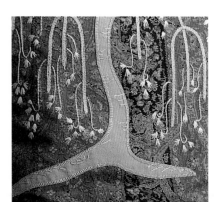
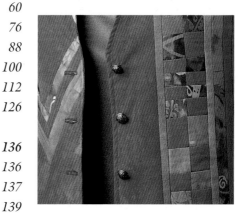

INTRODUCTION

A VEST MAY JUST BE the single most perfect garment. It's appropriate for all occasions, and it can be flattering to every body configuration. It adapts to a full range of personal styles, from ultra-conservative to utterly flamboyant. And it adjusts in a minute to fashion's latest whims.

A vest can make a quick and significant change to your overall look. If your wardrobe's mainstay is an excellent but less-than-exciting suit, a striking vest will give it new life. For a wardrobe based on jeans and white shirts, a bright vest or two can be great extenders. If you're a person who enjoys keeping up with the very latest trends, the addition of a vest in this season's color/length/fabric can render your entire closet *au courant*.

Vests have their practical side too. When padded with down, cotton batting, or some technologically advanced insulation material, they add a layer of warmth around the torso. A vest provides a surface for the attachment of numerous extra pockets—a boon to equipment-intensive vocations such as fishing, photography, or gardening.

ALWAYS IN STYLE

VESTS OR SOME VARIATION of them have been around for at least 28 centuries. Greek soldiers wore the ancestor of today's bulletproof vest in 800 B.C. It was made of leather or articulated metal plates designed to soften the blows of enemy swords. In ancient Asia, padded vests were worn as undergarments.

On the fashion scene, the vest, the waistcoat, and their kin have long had a place in both men's and women's wardrobes. Men's waistcoats have supplied the third piece of a suit for hundreds of years. In the eighteenth and nineteenth centuries, these were elaborately decorated to replicate the style of the outer coat. Women wore long vestlike garments over full-skirted dresses. Women's sportswear, such as riding clothes, often was modeled after the outfits worn by men for the same purpose and often included vests.

During America's colonial days, clothing styles followed the current European trends of the time, and men's suits featured ornate, lavishly embroidered vests. Quakers during that period wore suits of the same cut but without the embellishment, a simplified style not far removed from today's conservative corporate suits.

Men's waistcoat typical of the 1770s.

6

In the West, practicality took precedence over fashion. Cowhide and deerskin were more readily available than fine embroidered wool, and they offered better protection against the elements. American Indians adorned leather vests with elaborate beadwork, initiating a style that is still popular.

During World War II, with wool inventories diverted to the manufacture of uniforms, a restriction was imposed on tailors limiting the amount of wool that could go into a suit, and vests were excluded. Since that time, and perhaps because of that interval of deprivation, vests have been part of the fashion scene almost continuously.

Today's vests continue in their historic roles—giving protection, providing warmth, and supplying the socially correct third element of a formal suit. We've added a few new reasons to wear them too. They add a touch of whimsy to the wardrobe, allow us to indulge in flights of fancy, commemorate a special occasion, or broadcast a message. Most of all, they're fun!

colored machine embroidery may be unappealing, a vest decorated in this way looks perfectly appropriate. A patchwork jacket may not quite fit your image, yet a patchwork vest could be very handsome. A vest is a good excuse for color experimentation too. If you love bright green but it clashes with your complexion, it could be used judiciously on a vest without ill effect.

Since a vest takes so little fabric, it's a wonderful opportunity to use luxurious fabrics that may be unaffordable in the quantity needed for a dress or jacket.

Even a sewer with limited experience can put together a sensational vest. A piece of great fabric, a free evening, and *voilà*, you have a snappy new accent for tomorrow's outfit. Many of the vests shown on the following pages *were* made by pros, but many others, wonderful others, were made by people with little sewing knowledge and great imagination.

If you've never sewn at all and want to give it a try, a vest is an ideal beginner's garment. Keep your first one simple, and your success will encourage you to create a more elaborate design next time.

Sioux beaded vest from the 1890s.

SEWING YOUR OWN VESTS

FOR THOSE WHO ENJOY SEWING, a vest allows unlimited creative expression. Its small surface provides a wonderful place to experiment with an untried technique. While an entire skirt adorned with bold-

Everything you need is here: a pattern, step-by-step sewing instructions, and plenty of tips on embellishment techniques. Let these designers' vests inspire you to create magnificent designs of your own!

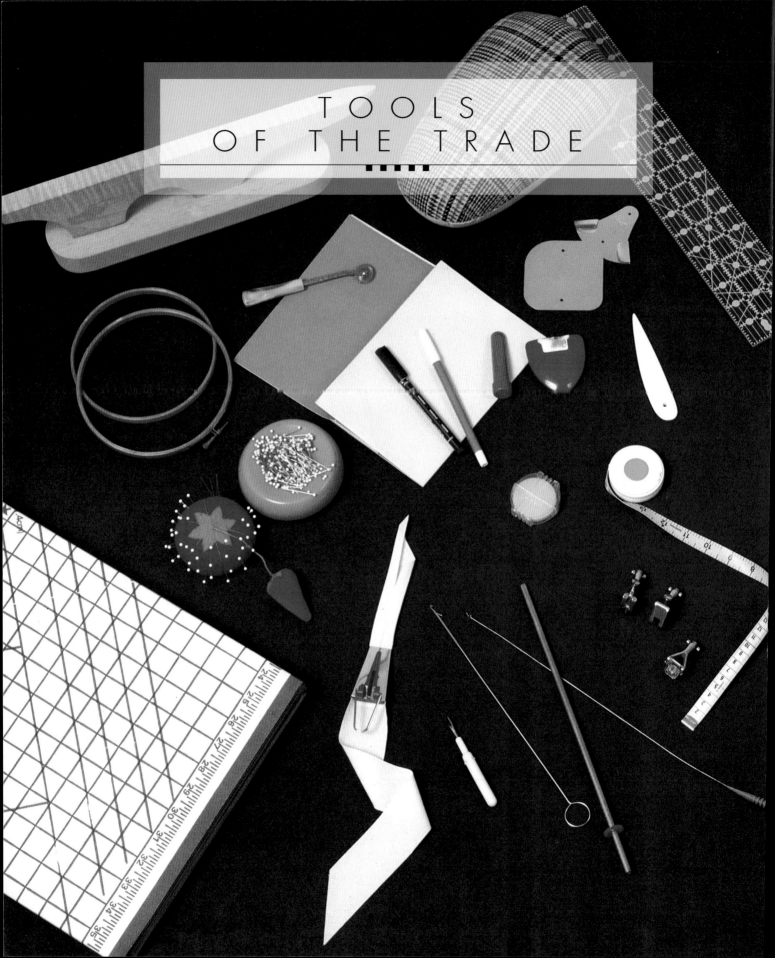

TOOLS
OF THE TRADE

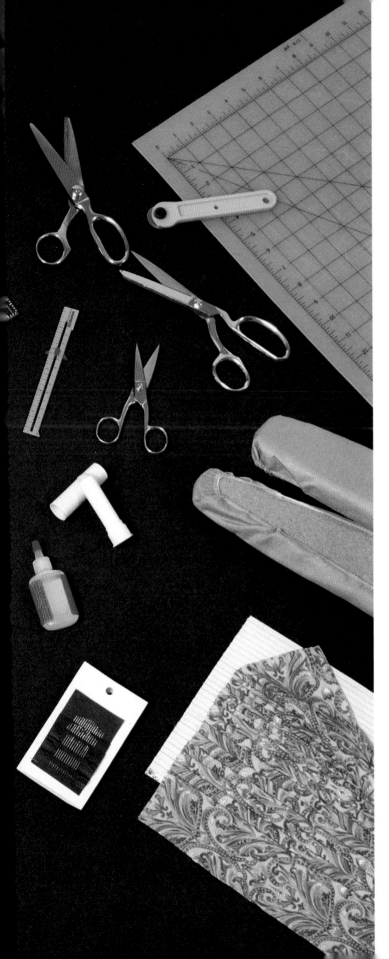

A WELL-EQUIPPED, COMFORTABLE SEWING AREA adds to the enjoyment of a sewing project. Every sewer has a different list of essential tools and notions, and probably no two lists are alike. Some of the equipment and accessories included below are unquestionably essential; some are merely very handy to have for certain techniques.

SEWING MACHINE

WHETHER YOUR MACHINE is the state-of-the art model or one inherited from your mother, it will do the job if its needs are met. First and foremost, the upper thread and bobbin tensions should be adjusted to give an even line of stitching without puckering. If your attempts to correct tension problems aren't successful, take your machine to the dealer.

The machine should be cleaned and oiled regularly, according to the instructions in the manual. A build-up of crud will affect the stitching sooner or later, and a sewing machine without oil works about as well as does a car without oil.

The most important part of your machine is the needle. It is essential to replace the needle regularly, and it's a good idea to change it after every project. Use the needle type specified in your instruction manual, with the size and point style appropriate for the fabric you are sewing.

9

Sewing tools and equipment.

Opposite page, left to right in rows: point presser, pressing ham, plastic ruler, embroidery hoop, dressmaker's carbon and tracing wheel, water-soluble marker (blue), water-proof marker (black), two types of powdered chalk marker, pocket template, point turner, glass-headed pins in an old-fashioned pincushion and a magnetic holder, beeswax, tape measure, cutting board, bias tape maker, seam ripper, two different tube turners, three special sewing machine feet—buttonhole, piping, and clear appliqué.

This page, left to right in rows: pinking shears, rotary cutter and mat, dressmaker's shears, seam gauge, trimming scissors, glue stick, sleeve board, liquid fray retardant, assortment of hand sewing needles, pleater.

Presser feet designed for specific techniques perform those tasks with ease and success. The vest-making projects in this book include techniques for which these feet are helpful: cording, piping, appliqué, satin stitch, freehand embroidery or darning, and the even-feed or walking foot. Other feet may be available for your own machine or for techniques that you use frequently.

SERGER

THE SERGER REQUIRES the same attention to needles and oiling as does a sewing machine, and it needs cleaning even more frequently. Knife blades must be sharp and free of nicks to cut smoothly.

PRESSING EQUIPMENT

A GOOD STEAM IRON—one that doesn't drip—is as important to sewing as the sewing machine itself. Steam pressing sets the stitching lines and helps shape your garment. A leaky iron, or one that sputters, will leave water spots on some fabrics, especially bright-colored silks and fabrics containing acetate.

In addition to a standard ironing board, the following tools help you get professional-looking results when you press a garment.

Ham. As its name suggests, this is a rounded cushion used for pressing curved seams and darts.

Sleeve board. Not just for sleeves, this mini-ironing board is useful for any small area.

Pressing cloth. A soft, clean pressing cloth is essential for ironing delicate fabrics and for fusing interfacings.

Point presser. This is a narrow wooden pressing board, often attached to a stand called a clapper. A point presser is handy for dealing with hard-to-reach seams, and it allows you to press a seam open without leaving an imprint on the right side of the fabric.

The clapper is used to pound steam into fabrics, such as wool, that do not make a crisp edge easily.

Pocket template. It serves as a pressing guide to make pockets or other corners neat and symmetrical.

CUTTING TOOLS

Cutting board. Made of heavy cardboard and printed with a grid, it's used for straightening and cutting fabric.

Dressmaker's shears. Make sure that you have good sharp ones, keep them hidden from children, and never use them to cut anything but fabric.

Rotary cutter and mat. A rotary cutter is fast and accurate, especially when making straight cuts and when working with slippery lining fabrics. The mat provides a cutting surface that won't dull the cutter.

Pinking shears. These are nice for finishing seams, especially in garments that are lined, where overcast seams would be overly bulky.

Trimming scissors. A pair with short, pointed blades is useful for all sorts of trimming and essential for embroidery and other detailed needlework.

MEASURING AND MARKING DEVICES

Seam gauge. This short ruler, with its adjustable marker, is perfect for measuring seams and hems.

Tape measure. A flexible tape measure is invaluable for measuring yourself and your pattern.

Ruler. You don't need anything fancy, just a clear plastic one to use with a rotary cutter.

Carpenter's square. This is an L-shaped metal ruler that's handy for making pattern alterations

Powdered chalk marker. A plastic container filled with powdered chalk, it's used for marking fine lines.

Water-soluble fabric marking pen. It's used for temporary markings; the ink is removed with a damp

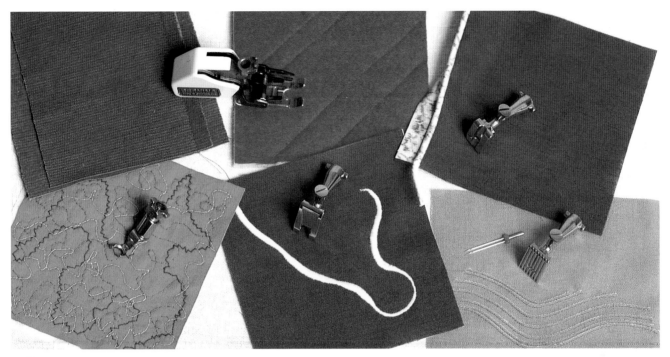

Special presser feet, in rows left to right: even-feed (walking) foot for sewing multiple layers and fabrics that scoot; piping foot; freehand embroidery foot; open embroidery foot for free-motion stitching; pintuck foot, shown with double-needle tucks.

cloth and can even be obliterated with a wet finger. Always test a marking pen on a fabric scrap—some fabric dyes make the ink difficult to remove.

Waterproof marking pen. This more permanent marker is used for indicating pattern alterations and for tracing appliqué.

NOTIONS AND GADGETS

Pins. The long, sharp, glass-headed ones are best.

Hand sewing needles. Small needles work best for most hand sewing; use larger ones for heavier fabrics. Assortments that include sharps, embroidery needles, and darners are inexpensive and readily available.

Beeswax. Waxing hand sewing thread can reduce tangling. Be sure the wax doesn't mark your fabric when the stitching is pressed.

Thimble. A thimble should fit snugly onto your mid-dle finger, where it will save wear and tear on your skin as you sew by hand. Once you get accustomed to using it, a thimble will speed your sewing.

Seam ripper. It should have a razor-sharp blade to function properly; a dull seam ripper can damage your fabric.

Glue stick or fabric glue. For quick basting, it can be a neat substitute for needle and thread.

Tube turner. The best kind has a hollow metal tube into which a spiral-tipped wire is inserted to pull the fabric through. For very narrow tubes, the long latch-hook turner works well.

Point turner. This is a plastic or wooden tool that helps turn a perfect point.

Bias tape makers. They come in several sizes and are used to fold bias strips of fabric for edge binding.

Liquid fray retardant. A colorless liquid, it prevents raveling along fabric edges and reinforces closely clipped corners.

SELECTING YOUR FABRIC

THE LOOK OF A GARMENT greatly depends on the fabric used to make it. It's not only a matter of the fabric's beauty, but whether the fabric is compatible with the garment style. Inside fabrics are equally important; interfacing, underlining, and lining give the garment its ultimate shape and allow it to drape in an attractive fashion.

Every fabric has built-in characteristics that determine how it will perform as a garment. Each has a unique "hand," or feel. Each drapes in a particular way, responds differently to shaping, and has a different degree of crispness or softness. Fabrics all have their own care requirements, and every one wears differently with regard to wrinkling, breathability, and comfort in extreme temperatures.

A little fabric savvy will help you make the best choice for the design you plan, and it will reward you with an attractive and comfortable garment. To start with, a fabric is classified by three different means: by the way in which it is constructed, by the weave or surface patterning, and by the fiber from which it is made.

Generally speaking, fabrics are either woven or knitted. Knit fabrics—jersey, sweater woolens, polyester double knits, whatever—are all constructed using the same technique, regardless of the fiber used for them. Because the collection of vests in this book includes neither hand knits nor any made of knitted fabric, there's no further elaboration on knits here.

Woven fabrics vary greatly in appearance, but all are formed by interlacing vertical strands (warp) with horizontal ones (weft). They are often identified by their weave structure and/or surface texture, with terms such as gabardine, satin,

velvet, and crepe. Gabardine, for example, might be made of wool, silk, polyester, or rayon. The word "gabardine" refers to the fabric's twill weave structure, not to the fiber from which it is made. "Gabardine" explains the appearance of the fabric, but doesn't tell you how (or whether) the fabric is to be laundered, whether it will wrinkle, or how hot an iron to use when pressing it.

From a sewer's point of view, the fiber content of a fabric is its most important feature. The type of fiber is what determines how to treat a fabric during construction, how to press it, how it will look and behave in your garment, and the kind of care the finished piece will require. Fibers are the raw materials from which fabrics are made.

Fabric fibers are classified, according to their origin, either as natural or man-made. Natural fibers originate from plants and animals—cotton, linen, ramie, silk, and wool. Man-made or synthetic fibers, such as polyester, nylon, and acrylic, are made from chemical compounds. A "blend" can be any combination of fibers making up a fabric, but it most often refers to the combination of a natural fiber with a synthetic.

Below are brief descriptions of fabric fibers and their characteristics, along with some of the fabrics associated with each kind.

NATURAL FIBERS

FABRICS MADE FROM NATURAL FIBERS have aesthetic qualities that cannot be duplicated synthetically. Natural fiber fabrics are usually easier to work with than synthetics. Most are obedient and responsive to shaping. Natural fibers also breathe better than synthetics, making them cooler to wear in warm weather and warmer in cold weather.

Let your imagination go when choosing fabrics, or even making your own, for your vest. In the vest in the foreground, solid-colored cotton provides a dramatic contrast to complex Peruvian weaving. The fabrics for the other two vests are more unusual: the blue one is made of strips of ikat-weave silk that have been woven together, and the "fabric" for the red one is actually embroidered cotton ribbon alternating with red grosgrain.

Virtually all natural fiber fabrics are washable, even wool and most silks. Unfortunately, nearly all will shrink in the process. These fabrics must be preshrunk if they are to be used in garments or other items that will later be washed. Washing will also remove the finishes used, most noticeably those on heavier silks.

Ready-to-wear garments made of natural fibers are often labeled "dry clean only" for several reasons. First, most manufacturers rarely preshrink their fabrics. In addition, the interfacings and linings used in manufactured clothing often are of a lesser quality and have greater shrinkage potential than the outer garment fabrics. Finally, manufacturers have little faith in the average consumer's laundry skills, and they must protect themselves.

■ Cotton ■

COTTON IS THE MOST VERSATILE of all fibers. Cotton fabrics are available in every conceivable weave and finish, in every texture and weight, and in every price range. Cotton fabrics are easy to sew and press and are adaptable to almost any sewing technique. Cotton often is blended with other fibers, such as polyester, to reduce wrinkling, but the blends lack the responsive qualities of pure cotton fabrics.

All cottons are washable, although almost all of them will shrink to a greater or lesser degree. They should always be washed before use. Some cottons, especially lower priced varieties and those intended for use in home decorating, are treated with a finishing agent, such as starch, to give them smoothness and stability. Washing removes the finish, leaving the fabric softer, less smooth, and with less body.

Many different cotton fabrics are used for the vests in this book. Those listed below deserve special mention.

Batiste and *lawn* are very lightweight, even-weave cottons. They are beautiful in their own right and make exceptionally good support fabrics when used as underlining.

Flannel, or *flannelette*, is a lightweight fabric with a pronounced nap on one side. It tends to shrink considerably and should be machine washed and dried at least once before cutting. When used as an underlining, cotton flannel adds body to light- or medium-weight cottons and gives dimension to quilted garments.

Indian cotton is a broad term that refers to lightweight fabrics made from short-staple cotton fibers. They are cool and comfortable in hot weather and are quite inexpensive. Usually heavily finished, they will become softer and less stable after washing. Preshrinking is essential.

Muslin is a very versatile, very inexpensive, and highly underrated fabric that is well suited to dyeing, fabric manipulation, and all sorts of embellishment. And it's available in almost any fabric store. Don't be deceived by its initial stiffness; it develops an interesting texture when washed and machine dried.

Organdy is a sheer, firm cotton with a built-in crispness that makes it an excellent interfacing where support is needed, such as in shirt collars and under buttonholes.

Pima is the Rolls Royce of cottons. It has a silky hand and almost whistles when stroked. It is made from a variety of the cotton plant that produces long fibers, and it's more expensive to produce than other cottons. Pima cotton fabrics tend to be crisper and more stable (i.e., they wrinkle and shrink less) than fabrics made from short-staple cottons.

Polished cotton is a plain-weave cotton, such as broadcloth, that has been chemically finished to give it sheen and crispness. The finish will not withstand laundering, but it may last through several dry cleanings. *Chintz* is a polished cotton that is usually printed with a floral pattern.

Sateen has a sheen similar to that of polished cotton, but in sateen it is due to the satin weave of the fabric, not to finishing agents. Sateen retains its lustrous appearance after washing.

Velvet, or *velveteen*, is widely available made of cotton, although it's also made of rayon, silk, and wool. Cotton velvets do not have the draping qualities of rayon and silk but are easier to sew. They're also less expensive and, in some cases, are washable.

■ Linen ■

LINEN IS THE FIBER of the flax plant, which produces an extremely strong and durable fabric. Because of the complicated manufacturing process required, linen is often fairly expensive. It's a very comfortable summer

14

fabric, since it breathes very well and dries quickly.

Linen ages gracefully; the more it is used and laundered, the softer and more lustrous it becomes. White or natural-colored linens can withstand washing in hot water with bleach, but dyed linens should be treated more gently to keep their colors from fading.

Linen *will* wrinkle—it's that very quality that separates the real thing from the imitations. Linen that is washed wrinkles in a different way from linen that is dry cleaned. Washing leaves linen softer and somewhat rumply. New linen fabric, or that which is dry cleaned, creases instead. Even with wrinkles, linen has a distinctive and handsome appearance that no synthetic can match.

Linen is available in many textures and weights. The lightweight, smooth-textured variety is sometimes called "handkerchief linen," although what's sold under that name usually is not the fabric used for hankies. Heavier linen often has slubs and a rougher texture, giving it the characteristic "linen weave" we associate with the fabric. Linen is the *fiber,* however, not the weave. There is no such thing as "synthetic linen." Fabrics labelled "linen weave" invariable are *not* linen, but are often a rayon/polyester blend. Beyond appearance, from a distance at least, the two fabrics have nothing in common.

Linen should be prewashed at least once if it is to become a washable garment. It's a good idea to machine dry the fabric to preshrink it, then line dry the finished garment. Many sewers have linen fabric dry cleaned before making it into a garment that will be dry cleaned.

■ Ramie ■

RAMIE IS A FIBER TAKEN from a plant native to Asia. It produces a fabric that is similar to linen but somewhat coarser and not quite as durable. It is also less costly. It can be treated in the same way as linen or cotton, and

it's usually blended with one or the other in fabrics. Ramie is in no way related to rayon, by the way.

■ Silk ■

SILK FIBERS PRODUCE FABRICS that are unsurpassed for elegance and luxurious appearance. Some silk fabrics have an inherent stiffness that allows them to drape and fold in a distinctive way, many are very soft and light, and others are rough-textured and heavy. No matter what its weight or texture, silk is comfortable to wear. The lightweight varieties feel delicious next to the skin.

Silk doesn't have a good "memory." It may stretch but not return to its original shape. A shaped silk garment, such as a vest, does well when underlined with very light fusible interfacing— a tricot or weft-insertion type—or with a rayon cool-fuse variety.

Lighter weight silks, such as crepe, charmeuse, and noil, wash beautifully and become softer with time. They will shrink, so the fabric must be preshrunk to make a washable garment.

Silk should be washed with a gentle soap, not a detergent. The best one to use is a livestock shampoo, available at farm supply stores and from quilting and yarn suppliers. Regular shampoo, without conditioner or the like, works well too.

Because silk doesn't hold dye well, dark or bright colors may fade or run when washed. These should be dry cleaned to keep the colors intact or, if washed, washed alone. Heavy silks also should be dry cleaned to retain their finishing agents.

With lightweight silks, take care to sew with a perfect machine needle to avoid damaging the fabric. Most require a small needle size.

Almost any silk fabric can create an elegant vest, and silk is one of the most popular fabrics with the designers whose vests are shown in the photos. Characteristics of the different silk fabrics are given below.

Charmeuse is a soft, lightweight reversible fabric with a

15

satin finish on one side and crepe on the other. If washed, it resists wrinkling. It's probably not the best choice for a vest because of the extent to which it drapes; charmeuse requires a backing to shape it.

China silk or ***habutae*** is also known as lining silk and for that purpose is excellent. It's too fragile to use alone; the seams may pull out.

Crêpe de Chine is a lightweight fabric with a crepe texture and a tendency to drape easily. Like charmeuse, it doesn't wrinkle once it's washed, but instead develops a lovely crumpled surface texture. It works well in a patchwork vest, as shown on page 104, with a backing such as cotton lawn or flannel.

Matka is a heavier, even-weave silk with a surface texture almost like burlap. It's a very good vest fabric that is best when underlined with a lightweight fusible material to help it retain its shape. Matka silks should be dry cleaned.

Noil, also erroneously known as raw silk, is made with the short silk fibers left over from spinning the long fibers into the more expensive silk fabrics. Consequently it is quite inexpensive relative to other silks. Noil is one of the most versatile fabrics there is. It has a good, medium weight; after washing it won't wrinkle and requires little pressing; furthermore, it is very comfortable to wear. For a vest it should be backed with a light sew-in interfacing, such as cotton flannel or lawn. If it is to be heavily embroidered, a featherweight fusible would work well.

Raw silk is made from silk fibers that have not been processed to remove the natural gum. It has a characteristically uneven texture and is most often seen in its natural rich brown shades. It is a heavier silk and should be treated like matka.

Sandwashed silk can be any lighter weight silk fabric that has undergone a process to give it a slightly suedelike surface texture and gently faded color. It's luscious to wear, washes beautifully, and rarely needs pressing. Beware of sandwashed habutae;

although the process makes the fabric feel thicker, it is essentially the same delicate habutae. Sandwashed silks still should be preshrunk before use.

Silk linen is a heavier silk with a linen-weave texture. Its characteristics are similar to those of matka.

■ Wool ■

WOOL FABRICS ARE EXCELLENT for sewing because they can be shaped easily, and they hold their shape well. Wool is available in every conceivable weave, texture, and finish. Because the fabric breathes, wool is comfortable to wear in all but extremely warm and humid weather.

Wool resists wrinkles, and contrary to popular belief, most woolens wash beautifully. Wool *must* be preshrunk before sewing if the finished product will be laundered. It should be washed in cool to tepid water, since either extremely hot or extremely cold water will cause the fibers to mat and felt. Like silk, it is best washed with soap, such as a livestock shampoo.

SYNTHETIC FIBERS

IN GENERAL, fabrics made from man-made fibers are durable, washable, and wrinkle-resistent. Synthetic fibers are used for every kind of fabric weave and texture, including some that resemble natural fiber fabrics in appearance.

Most synthetic fabrics are quite stable—they don't tend to stretch out of shape, which also means that they have little "ease" and cannot be shaped and molded as well as natural fiber fabrics can. Most synthetics are less expensive than their natural fiber counterparts, and the two are often blended together to produce economical fabrics.

Changes and improvements in synthetic fibers occur hourly, and for this reason it is especially important with synthetic fabrics to follow the manufacturers' guidelines for dry cleaning or washing and pressing. Some are sensitive to heat and will pucker or melt with the touch of a too-hot iron. Some will yellow if washed with chlorine bleach. Others are affected by certain chemicals: nail polish remover will dissolve acetate, for example.

Below are characteristics of some of the man-made fibers most widely available in yard goods.

■ Acetate ■

ACETATE IS A CRISP, fairly stiff fabric with considerable sheen. When unblended it is used primarily for lining. It is often blended with cotton in faille and moiré-patterned fabrics. It is prone to fading from sunlight, perspiration, and dry cleaning. Fabrics containing acetate should not be washed, and they are prone to water spotting.

■ Polyester ■

OF ALL THE MAN-MADE FIBERS, polyester is probably the most widely used. It is extremely durable and is available in every conceivable weave and texture. Polyester fabrics wash well, with little or no shrinkage, and dry quickly. They resent chlorine bleach—it will yellow a white fabric—and too hot an iron may cause puckering or shrinking. They retain their shape and resist wrinkling and fading. They don't breathe well, however, and can be uncomfortable to wear in temperatures of either extreme.

Often polyester is blended with natural fibers to give them strength and stability. The resulting blends are less expensive and easier to care for than the comparable natural fiber fabrics, but they can't be shaped

Mother and daughter: Mom's vest has a splendid mix of fabrics, including wool crepe, polyester, acetate, cotton sateen, and silk; her daughter's vest is made using just one fabric— satin acetate—in a rainbow of luminous colors.

and eased, nor do they wear in the same graceful way as their natural fiber counterparts.

Blends can be a confusing term. A blend can be any combination of fibers used to make up a fabric, such as cotton with ramie, or silk and wool. But the term is most often used to indicate a mix of synthetic and natural fibers. Always ask, "A blend of what?"

■ Rayon ■

RAYON IS SOMEWHAT of a hybrid, a man-made fiber from a natural substance. Rayon, like acetate, is made of cellulose but by a different process. Rayon fabrics are very soft and fluid, and they have an attractive sheen. Rayon is not strong, and it doesn't hold its shape well, making it most suitable for flowing garment styles rather than shaped ones. It is often combined with fabrics that are stronger and more stable, such as cotton or polyester. Most rayons and rayon blends should be dry cleaned.

WHERE TO FIND THE PERFECT FABRIC

THE LOGICAL PLACE, of course, is in fabric stores. Those that sell good quality fabrics usually also have knowledgeable employees who are willing to help you with fabric selection and any specific sewing problems. Interesting vest fabrics can come from some unusual sources too. If you lack expertise where fabrics are concerned, be careful about what you buy. A mystery fabric can produce some unpleasant surprises after it is made into a garment. My policy is to throw such a treasure into the washing machine. If it is going to disintegrate in the wash, it's better to know this ahead of time, not after hours have been spent creating a garment.

■ Mill-end and outlet stores ■

EVERYONE LOVES BARGAINS, and some great ones can be found in stores that feature mill overruns and end cuts from manufacturers and designers. Check these fabrics for flaws and stains.

■ Home-decorating shops ■

SOME TAPESTRY AND CHINTZ fabrics make beautiful vests. Fabrics intended for decorating use are usually given chemical finishes to stabilize them, to make them stain and soil resistant, and to add surface sheen. The finishing agents will wash out, but washing may drastically alter the appearance and hand of the fabric. Washing will soften them too, making them more suitable for use in garments.

■ Grandmother's attic ■

IT'S FUN TO MAKE a garment that has history sewn in, and really good quality fabrics used to be more affordable and readily available than they are now. Old linens, old suits and dresses, and perhaps your own christening blanket all can be converted to unique garments.

■ Someone else's grandmother's attic ■

ESTATE SALES, FLEA MARKETS, consignment shops, yard sales, antique shops, and the like can supply wonderful vintage fabrics, and not necessarily in the form of clothing. Draperies and curtains rescued from older homes, dresser scarves, embroidered linens, crocheted pieces, and handmade lace all have superb potential. The chapter on vests made from recycled materials should give you plenty of ideas.

■ The back of your closet ■

THERE IS SURELY SOME RECYCLING potential there! Almost every other garment in the closet is bigger than a vest; therefore, any of them can *become* a vest. If you've always found it painful to part with favorite old garments, here's a pleasant alternative.

*When attaching heavy decorations, such as buttons, to your vest,
a firm backing is required to prevent the outer fabric from sagging out of shape.*

F A B R I C S   F O R   L I N I N G S

A GARMENT LINING serves several purposes. It allows the garment to slip on easily and to be worn without clinging forlornly to the clothing beneath it. It hides construction details, and it helps prevent wrinkles. In the case of a vest, making one with a lining is easier than making one without! A lining also adds considerable value to the look of any garment.

A lining can also be decorative, making a statement of its own. The photographs of the vests included in this book don't often show the linings, but some of the more unusual and interesting ones are mentioned in the accompanying text just to give you some ideas.

Some fabrics are made especially to be used for linings. The best ones are good quality polyester, Bemberg rayon, and China silk. Poor quality polyester linings can shrink if ironed with a hot iron (i.e., don't use them in a linen vest), but good polyester lining withstands more ironing. Rayon is fussy about washing, so it is best used in hand washable or dry cleanable garments. It too resents a hot iron. China silk is a luxurious lining that will make you smile every time you put on your garment. If used in something that you want to be washable, it must be preshrunk. It too should not be pressed with a hot iron. China silk is a bit more expensive than good rayon lining, but since a vest requires so little lining fabric, it's worth the extra investment!

Acetate is a traditional fabric for lining, but it's not especially comfortable to wear. Nor does it age well. Not only is it given to color fading for no apparent reason, but dry cleaning it often results in a tie-dyed look. Because of its tendency to water spot, acetate is not washable. Overall, its best quality is its low price.

The advantage to traditional lining fabrics is that they're slick, thus easy to wear, and that they're generally less expensive than "fashion" fabrics. For a less conservative approach, consider that some of the best lining fabrics are not designed to be lining fabrics at all. About the only rules you need to follow are that the lining should not be heavier or stiffer than the outer fabric, and that the two fabrics should be compatible as far as washability and ironing are concerned. Otherwise, anything goes! In most cases, no one but you will see it unless you want them to, so have fun with the inside and please yourself.

Nontraditional linings include fabrics from articles of clothing that are no longer worn for one reason or another. One of my favorite vests is lined with a beloved old shirt, the cut of which screamed "fifteen years old," but the fabric was beautiful pima cotton. It makes a splendid vest lining. Another option is to pair wild prints on the inside with plain outer fabric. Add your own "signature" by decorating the lining with a miniature of a design that appears on the outside. These little details make your vest a pleasure to wear.

Traditional vests—those functioning as the third piece of a man's three-piece suit—have backs made of lining fabric. Since these vests are intended to be worn under coats, the thinking is, why waste the expensive wool? Using the thinner lining fabric for the back also makes the ensemble more comfortable.

UNDERLINING

FABRICS INSIDE A GARMENT, hidden from view once construction is complete, can affect a vest's appearance as much as the outer fabric or lining. One of the most overlooked inside fabrics is the underlining.

Underlining is cut to the size and shape of the pattern pieces, then either basted or bonded to the wrong side of the outer fabric. The two pieces are then treated as one throughout the rest of the construction process. Underlining has several functions. It improves the appearance of your vest by adding body to the outer fabric, which makes the garment look richer and reduces wrinkling. It serves as a backing for embroidery, appliqué, and other stitchery that would cause puckering in the fashion fabric alone. When using fashion fabrics that are somewhat translucent, an underlining prevents show-through of seam allowances and construction details.

Almost any lightweight fabric can be used as underlining. The fabric should be at least as light in weight as the outer fabric, and it should drape in the same way. Equally important, it should have the same care requirements.

Lightweight and featherweight interfacing fabrics often are used as underlinings, especially fusible interfacings such as tricot and the weft-insertion varieties. Because the two are actually bonded together, fusible underlinings will change the character of the outer fabric to some degree. This can be desirable with fabrics such as heavy silk, which requires underlining for shape retention.

If your vest will be made of a natural fiber fabric, it's best to use a natural fiber fabric for a sew-in underlining. Cotton lawn and batiste work well with many fabrics, and muslin is fine with medium to heavy ones. To determine what will work, hold the two fabrics together to see how they drape and how they feel together. With fusibles, test if possible to be sure the resulting bonded fabric doesn't have more stiffness than you expected.

Here are some examples of underlining and outer fabric combinations that work well:

- Cotton flannel with lightweight cotton prints, especially if there will be quilting.
- Cotton batiste with lightweight linen, wool challis or gabardine, or lightweight cotton.
- Cool-fuse rayon with medium-weight cotton or silk.
- Featherweight weft-insertion fusible interfacing with matka silk or silk linen.
- Cotton muslin with medium to heavy cotton.

Whatever fabric is used, it must be preshrunk along with the outer garment fabric. The process for testing and preshrinking fusible fabrics is explained at the end of the interfacing section, below.

INTERFACING

THE INTERFACING IN A GARMENT adds stability where it's needed. In a vest, this is most often along the front edges behind the buttons and buttonholes. It may also be beneficial around the neck, lower front, and armholes, especially when using a very soft, fluid outer fabric. Many of the fabrics made for interfacing also can be used for underlining, as described above.

The vast numbers and kinds of interfacing materials now available are staggering. As new fabrics arrive on the scene, new interfacings are developed to back them up. If you're inexperienced at matching interfacing to fabric, find a good fabric store and ask their recommendations for your particular fabric and project.

Interfacings are divided into two broad categories: fusible (iron-on) and sew-in. They are also available in different weights, from featherweight to quite stiff. Following are descriptions of some basic types.

Woven interfacings may be all cotton or a poly/cotton blend. They are quite stable, and they're available in light to heavy weights. Wovens may be sew-in or fusible. These are probably not the best fabrics to use for underlining in a vest, but they would work well for front interfacing.

Nonwovens are made of a fibrous material and come in many forms and weights. Some are all-bias, meaning that they stretch in all directions. They are available as fusibles or sew-in. With these interfacings particularly, don't stint on quality. The bargain varieties can shred after one or two washings, ruining the garment in which you've invested many hours.

Tricot knit interfacings are usually fusible. Available in featherweight or lightweight types, they are quite soft and stretchy. These are good with fabrics that also have some stretch or drape.

Weft-insertion fusible interfacings also may be featherweight or lightweight. This is a knit/woven combination that is flexible, yet it provides stability.

Cool-fuse, or *temporary bond*, interfacings are hybrids. They press in place but don't actually bond to the fabric. As a result, they must be sewn into the seams. They are woven rayon, extremely light in weight, and work well even with lightweight silks.

Other fabrics that make excellent interfacing are cotton organdy, for medium to heavy cottons, and nylon chiffon, for lightweight fabrics that won't be subjected to a hot iron.

The interfacing question can be confusing to a novice sewer—it certainly is to the experienced ones! Your best bet is to test a sample of your

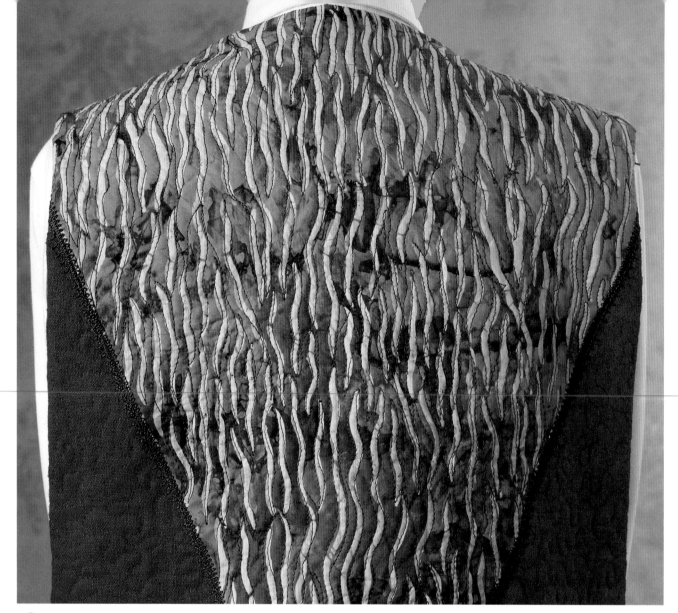

Garment-weight cotton or polyester batting provides a firm backing for the dense machine stitching used to quilt this vest.

proposed combination, particularly if you plan to use a fusible interfacing. If possible, wash the sample before sewing your vest. Manufacturers' instructions should be followed to the letter.

Even a fusible interfacing must be preshrunk, especially if it is used for a washable garment. Most of them will shrink. The result is the same as imperfect bonding: an unsightly bubbled appearance to the garment. To preshrink interfacing, first soak it for fifteen minutes or so in almost-hot water. Roll it in a towel, pressing it gently. Then, after smoothing out

any wrinkles, hang it to dry. Once it is dry, steam it, holding the iron a little above the fabric surface.

BACKING MATERIALS

WHEN A DESIGN CALLS for a considerable amount of stitching, such as a quilted pattern or one with elaborate machine embroidery, some fabrics may require backing. If left unbacked, the outer fabric may become puckered by the stitching. Backings, like other behind-the-scenes fabrics, should be compatible with the outer fabric in weight and care requirements.

Underlining can double as a backing if the outer fabric is not too light and the stitching not too dense. A lightweight fusible or firmly woven sew-in, such as organdy, will support moderate stitching on medium-weight fabric. Very light or unstable fabrics may require backing in addition to underlining. If appliqué or embroidery will be worked in a small, defined area, pieces of sew-in interfacing material, heavier than that used to underline the garment, can be used as backing under just the design areas.

Special backing fabrics are available expressly for use with machine embroidery and appliqué. For machine embroidery, there are nonwoven temporary (tear-away) backings that can be placed under the area to be embroidered. The excess can be torn away from around the embroidery after the stitching is finished. These backings are quite stiff. They will support any amount of heavy stitching without puckering, but they can also be too stiff to use with lightweight fabrics and are difficult to remove from between close lines of stitching. A paper-backed fusible web, made specifically for appliqué, allows designs to be traced and cut out, then bonded to the outer fabric. This, too, may provide more stiffness than is appropriate for some garment fabrics.

Water-soluble backings, which look like plastic and dissolve in contact with water, do well for lightweight fabrics and for designs with a moderate amount of stitching. Stitching lines can be drawn on them with a water-soluble pen, which will wash away also. In damp climates, this material should be stored in a tightly sealed moisture-proof container—humidity alone can sometimes dissolve it.

The best way to determine the right combination of backing and garment fabric is to test a sample. Layer the materials to be used—outer fabric, underlining, backing, everything—then test the stitching techniques on the sample to make sure that all are compatible and that they work together to produce the desired effect.

A WORD ABOUT THREADS

THERE ARE SEVERAL good kinds of thread for basic, non-decorative sewing. Decorative sewing threads are discussed in the section on machine embroidery, page 147.

Cotton-wrapped polyester is excellent for sewing most fabrics, and it's widely available. For very fine fabrics, such as sheer silk, it may be too heavy.

Polyester thread is somewhat finer and works well with thinner fabrics, yet it's strong enough for heavy fabrics too. It has a sheen that is sometimes undesirable with a dull-finished fabric such as soft cotton.

Polyester thread varies greatly in quality. Choose a name brand, and avoid the dozen-for-a-dollar bargains. Poor quality thread will break, knot, stretch, shear off at the needle's eye, and produce poor stitching. With sergers, it causes even greater problems.

How do you tell good thread from bad? Unwind about a half-yard (half-meter), and pull it through your fingers from the cut end (with the grain of the thread). It should feel smooth and have no lumps. Look at it closely. Good thread is evenly spun, with no thick or thin places and no fuzziness. The price difference between cheap thread and good thread is slight in comparison with the cost of fabric for a garment and the time invested in it.

All-cotton thread works especially well with cotton and wool fabrics, and it appeals to the purists. It's not widely available, however. Although it's manufactured by all the leading thread companies, few fabric stores stock it. Quality is as important with cotton thread as it is with polyester, and it can be determined in the same way. Because it's not as durable as polyester and cotton-wrapped polyester, all-cotton thread is probably not the best choice for garments that are subject to hard wear and much laundering.

CONSTRUCTING
A BASIC VEST

■■■■■

PREPARING THE PATTERN

THE VEST PATTERN is sized with generous ease and with low armholes to accommodate wide shirt sleeves. Because there is no such thing as standard sizing, the pattern should be measured for fit against a garment whose fit you like. Experienced sewers make a "muslin" from an untried pattern before cutting into the more expensive fabric. Make the test garment of muslin or any expendable fabric that's handy. Sew just the side and shoulder seams, and try on your "test" vest. While it may sound like a diversion from your goal of creating a beautiful vest, this step can save you a great deal of time in the long run.

The pattern should be enlarged to a 1" (2.5 cm) grid. A copy shop can do this, or the pattern can be redrawn at full size on gridded pattern-drafting material that is available from fabric and notions suppliers.

ALTERING THE PATTERN

CHANGES TO THE BASIC PATTERN can be made to improve the fit, change the style, or accommodate a particular design. Many alterations are easy to do if a few guidelines are followed.

- Work with a tracing or a copy of the full-size pattern to preserve your original.

- Pattern-drafting material, marked with a 1" (2.5 cm) grid, allows for accurate changes.

- Changes should be made from the seamlines, not the cutting lines. Draw in the seamlines on the pattern copy, and cut off the seam allowances. After

your changes have been made, add the seam allowances again.

- Make a muslin test garment to check any but the most minor changes.

- Use porous surgical tape (available in drugstores) rather than transparent tape for joining pattern pieces. It removes easily without tearing the paper, and it leaves no sticky residue.

■ Lengthening or shortening the vest ■

TO LENGTHEN, cut the pattern along the marked line. Move the pieces evenly apart, keeping the lengthwise grainline straight, and tape a piece of paper underneath. Then blend the side cutting lines.

To shorten the pattern, fold a pleat along the marked line. The pleat should equal half the amount by which the pattern needs to be shortened.

Be sure to lengthen or shorten the front and back equally. Remember to alter the interfacing pattern too, if you're using one.

The patterns for several of the vests shown in the project section were elongated to exaggerate the style (pages 63, 102, 105, and 113). This was done with two horizontal cuts: one as described above and a second one, parallel to the first, at the midpoint of the armhole.

■ Rounding off the front points ■

FOR A MORE CASUAL-LOOKING VEST, the front edges can be made rounded instead of pointed (see figure 1). The vests on pages 52, 131, and 134 illustrate a few examples of this style. Depending upon the

25

*Constructing a basic vest is simple, but the result doesn't
have to look plain. This one is beautifully decorated with heirloom lace and hand needlework.*

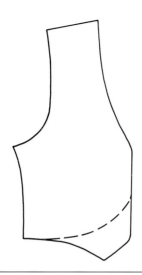

Figure 1. Rounding off the front points

effect you want, you can cut very little from the pattern and make subtle, rounded corners, or you can remove a substantial amount and have wide, flat curves. A bolero-style vest usually has wider curves, and the pattern is shortened to bring the bottom of the vest to or slightly above the waist.

■ Adding darts ■

IF YOU PREFER A MORE FITTED VEST, front and/or back darts can be added. First make up the vest in muslin. For front darts, extend lines downward from below the bust points on the lengthwise grain of the fabric, keeping them equidistant from the front edge. Pin the dart on the outside of the fabric; then baste and press. Back darts should be located under the shoulder blades, parallel to the center back. When the darts fit correctly, transfer the fold lines and stitching lines to the pattern pieces.

■ Raising the armhole ■

THE PATTERN HAS A LOWERED armhole to accommodate wide shirt sleeves. To raise the armhole, mark the side seamlines and draw lines *straight* upward to the desired underarm point. The new line should be parallel with the pattern's lengthwise grainline. Then

curve the line to blend with the original armhole line and with the side seamline at the point where the two lines diverged.

■ Collars ■

THE VEST ON PAGE 108 has an interesting half-collar, made by a simple extension of the front neck edge, as shown in figure 2. Add the seam allowance at the shoulder, and sew the upper edge of the collar into the shoulder seam.

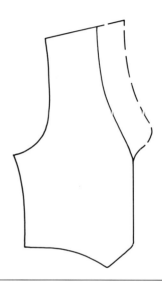

Figure 2. Adding a half-collar

To draft a full collar pattern, as in the vest on page 87, make a copy of the front and back pattern pieces, and tape them together at the shoulder *seamlines*. Draw in the seamline around neckline and front edges. Then draw the collar line as you want it to appear. (See figure 3.) Add seam allowances on all edges.

■ Princess seams ■

PRINCESS SEAMS on the vest front, as in the design on page 81, have a slimming effect and allow for creative fabric piecing besides. This pattern adjustment requires several steps to make, but it's not at all difficult. (Refer to figure 4.)

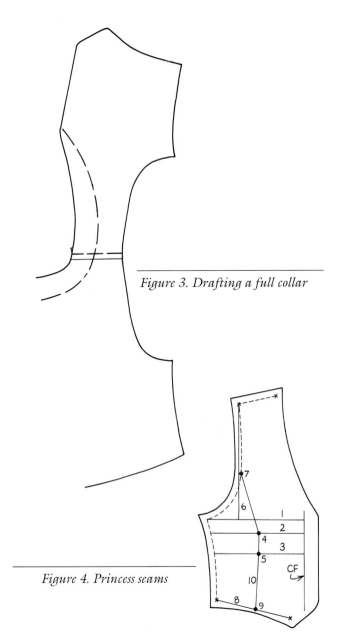

Figure 3. Drafting a full collar

Figure 4. Princess seams

side seamline and the center front.

5. Mark the same point on line 3.

6. Draw a line perpendicular to line 1, straight up from line 1 to the intersection of the shoulder/armhole seamlines. Measure this line.

7. Measure the total length of line 6. Measure up one-third of this distance on line 6 from line 1, and mark the point at the armhole seamline.

8. Draw a straight line from the intersection of the side/lower edge seamlines to the lower front point. Measure it.

9. Divide the line 8 measurement by 3. Measure by this distance from the front point on line 8 and mark that point.

10. Draw a straight line to connect the points marked in steps 4, 5, 7, and 9.

11. Round off the corners on line 10 to make a smooth curve. Extend the line across the seam allowances to the cutting lines.

12. Cut the pattern on this line. Trace the pieces onto paper, and add seam allowances to each of the cut edges.

When sewing this seam, first staystitch the concave curved edge to prevent stretching. Stitch along the edge in the seam allowance 1/16" (1.6 mm) from the seamline with a medium stitch length.

Before beginning, draw the seamlines on the front pattern piece at the shoulder and side, at the underarm/side corner, side/lower front corner, and the lower front point. Draw the center front line.

Mark and measure from the seamlines, not from the pattern edge.

1. Draw a line from the underarm to the center front, perpendicular to the center front.

2. Draw a line 1-1/4" (3.2 cm) below line 1.

3. Draw a line 2-1/4" (5.7 cm) below line 2.

4. On line 2, mark a point halfway between the

■ **Fabric Yardage Requirements** ■

AMOUNTS GIVEN IN THE CHART on page 28 are for the patterns as shown at the end of this chapter. If the length or width of the pattern is altered, the fabric requirement may differ. Lay out the altered pattern, and measure it to determine the amount of fabric that will be needed. Extra fabric may also be required for matching plaids or patterns and for adding pockets, belts, or other design features.

Two-way yardages are for fabrics that allow placement of the pattern pieces toward either cut end of the fabric. One-way yardages are for fabrics that require the tops of the pattern pieces all to be positioned toward the same cut end of the fabric. Examples of the latter are fabrics that have a nap, such as velvet or corduroy, and one-directional prints.

PREPARING THE FABRICS

FOR A VEST that will be washable, all fabrics—underlining, lining, and interfacings too—must be preshrunk. They should be washed, dried, and pressed in the same way that you intend to care for the finished garment. It's a good idea to preshrink washable lining and interfacing even when they will be used with an outer fabric that is not washable. For instructions on preshrinking fusible interfacings, see page 22.

ABOUT GRAINLINES— REQUIRED READING!

FOLLOWING THE GRAIN of the fabric is vital to creating the right look in your finished garment (see figure 5). The lengthwise grain is the direction parallel to the selvages, or finished side edges. The fabric stretches

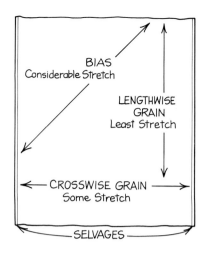

Figure 5. Fabric grainlines

least along the lengthwise grain, which is the reason the main garment pieces are always aligned this way. The cross grain is perpendicular to the lengthwise grain, or parallel to the torn or cut edge of the fabric. Most fabrics have some stretch in this direction.

The bias is the diagonal. True bias is a 45-degree angle between the lengthwise and crosswise grain lines, but any diagonal direction is considered bias. Fabric stretches most on the true bias but stretches considerably with any bias cut.

FABRIC WIDTH AND LENGTH REQUIRED YARDS (METERS)									
		36" (.9 m)		45" (1.1 m)		54" (1.4 m)		60" (1.5m)	
Pattern size:		ONE WAY	TWO WAY	ONE WAY	TWO WAY	ONE WAY	TWO WAY	ONE WAY	TWO WAY
Adult	XL	1-1/2 (1.4)	1-1/2 (1.4)	1-3/8 (1.3)	1-1/4 (1.1)	1-1/8 (1.0)	7/8 (.8)	1 (.9)	7/8 (.8)
	L	1-3/8 (1.3)	1-3/8 (1.3)	1-3/8 (1.3)	1-1/4 (1.1)	1-1/8 (1.0)	7/8 (.8)	7/8 (.8)	7/8 (.8)
	M	1-3/8 (1.3)	1-3/8 (1.3)	1-1/8 (1.0)	1 (.9)	7/8 (.8)	7/8 (.8)	7/8 (.8)	7/8 (.8)
	S	1-3/8 (1.3)	1-1/8 (1.0)	3/4 (.7)	3/4 (.7)	3/4 (.7)	3/4 (.7)	3/4 (.7)	3/4 (.7)
	XS	1-1/4 (1.1)	1-1/8 (1.0)	3/4 (.7)	3/4 (.7)	3/4 (.7)	3/4 (.7)	3/4 (.7)	3/4 (.7)
Child	L	1 (.9)	1 (.9)	3/4 (.7)	3/4 (.7)	3/4 (.7)	3/4 (.7)	3/4 (.7)	3/4 (.7)
	M	3/4 (.7)	5/8 (.6)	5/8 (.6)	5/8 (.6)	5/8 (.6)	5/8 (.6)	5/8 (.6)	5/8 (.6)
	S	1/2 (.5)	1/2 (.5)	1/2 (.5)	1/2 (.5)	1/2 (.5)	1/2 (.5)	1/2 (.5)	1/2 (.5)

28

DEALING WITH BIAS

ON THE VEST PATTERN, you can see that the front neckline and the front lower edges are all cut on the fabric bias to some degree. Except with very firmly woven fabrics, these areas can stretch, causing the front points to curl. This is a problem especially when the outer fabric and the lining have different degrees of stretchiness. Fortunately, there are several ways to counteract this tendency.

In the case of very stretchy fabrics, a lightweight fusible interfacing may be bonded to the outer vest fabric as soon as the pieces are cut. It's best in this case to apply interfacing to the vest back as well as the front for consistency.

For fabrics that aren't terribly stretchy, a tape stay should keep the edges in line. A tape made especially for this purpose is sheer but very firm and is available on rolls about 1/2" (1.3 cm) wide. In an emergency, the selvage cut from a firm lining fabric will serve the purpose.

Cut the length of tape stay to match the pattern seamline. Then, when attaching the lining, stitch the tape into the seams, easing the vest fabric to fit the stay.

Interfacing will work as a stabilizer for bias-cut areas too. Use the sew-in kind, in a weight appropriate for the vest fabric. Cut it from the vest front pattern, as shown in figure 6. After basting the inter-

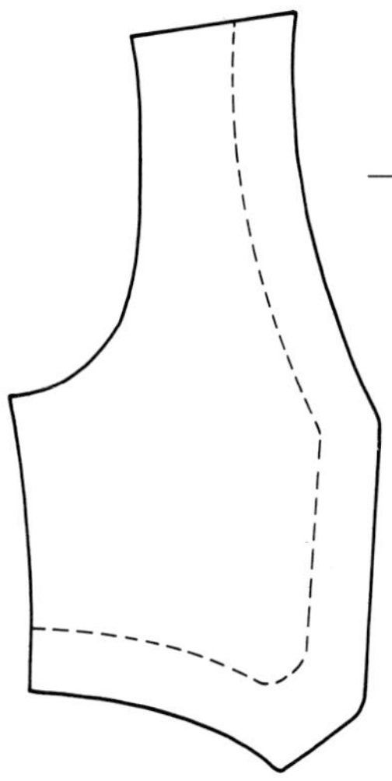

*Figure 6. Drafting
a pattern for interfacing*

facing to the vest front, sew it into the shoulder seams, the lining attachment seams, and the side seams.

Another method, often used for bias-cut skirts and the like, requires a little more patience but works well in cases where the fabric is quite stretchy and fusible interfacing is not desired. Sew the vest together at the shoulders, put it on a hanger and let it relax for several days. Then recut the front edges to the pattern.

For the less patient, one more alternative is to cut the lining fabric—which is usually the more stable—slightly longer at the lower front to allow the outer fabric some ease. In this case, a tape stay should be used at the neck edge.

BEFORE YOU CUT

ONCE YOU HAVE all your fabric preshrunk, it's natural to want to dive right in and cut out your pattern pieces. But wait! Before you start cutting, there are several things you need to decide—and a few that you may need to do.

29

- Decide whether you want to make any alterations to the pattern, either for size or style considerations (see page 24).

- Decide what kind of edging the vest will have (see page 143).

- Decide what kind of buttonholes you will use, if any (see page 139).

- Decide whether you will add a belt (see page 137).

- Decide whether you want a pocket (see page 153).

- All piecing, embroidery, and quilting should be completed *before* the vest pieces are trimmed to the pattern, as described in the instructions for those techniques.

Read about these options so that you can fit them into the construction process at the appropriate point.

CUTTING AND SEWING

ALL OF THE PATTERN LINES are cutting lines, and they include 5/8" (1.6 cm) seam allowances on all edges except at the center back. Seamlines are not indicated on the patterns; you may wish to mark your own with dotted lines.

Sew all seams with the right sides of the fabric together unless instructed otherwise. After it is sewn, press each seam. First press the stitching line; then press the seam open or to one side.

Grade all seam allowances to prevent their edges from showing through to the right side. Trim each layer of the seam allowance individually, cutting the least amount off the layer that lies against the outer fabric, and cutting the most off the layer farthest from the outer fabric.

Clip and notch any curved seams so that they will lie flat when the vest is turned right side out. On convex curves, such as the front points, cut V-shaped notches from the edge of the seam allowance almost to the stitching line. On concave curves, such as the armholes, clip almost to the seamline. (See figure 7.) Make clips or notches closer together on tight curves; for example, make them

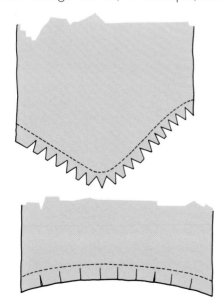

Figure 7. Notching convex curves and clipping concave curves

1/4" (6 mm) apart at the points and near the underarm seamline. On flatter curves, such as the front and back of the armhole, make clips 1/2" to 3/4" (about 1.5 to 2 cm) apart.

INSTRUCTIONS FOR MAKING A VEST

THE INSTRUCTION STEPS described below apply to most all vest designs. Instructions for optional features, such as belts and pockets, or for decorative techniques, such as embroidery and appliqué, are provided in the chapter on adding special touches, which begins on page 136.

This construction method is for a vest with outer edges topstitched or trimmed with piping. If you plan to bind the outer edges of your vest, follow the steps under Alternate Construction on page 31.

1. Cut two front sections, a right and a left, from the outer fabric, aligning the front edge of the pattern piece with the lengthwise grain of your fabric. Cut one back section on fabric folded along the lengthwise grain.

2. Cut the lining pieces the same way. Lightly mark the side seamline on the *right* side of each lining piece.

3. With right sides together, stitch the vest fronts to the back at the shoulders. Don't stitch the side seams yet.

4. Stitch the lining pieces in the same way.

5. To stabilize the bias edges, cut tape stays for the front edges, matching the seamlines of the pattern pieces from the shoulder to the side seams. Place the stays over the seamlines, and stitch 1/2" (1.3 cm) from the edge.

6. With right sides together, stitch the vest to the lining at the front edges and neck, around the armholes, and across the lower back, still leaving the side seams unsewn. Trim the seam allowances, especially at the corners. Then grade the seam allowances, leaving the lining seam allowance narrower than that of the outer fabric. As best you can, press the seam allowances toward the lining.

7. If the finished vest will not be topstitched or edgestitched, and piping trim is not used, understitch the seam allowances to the lining at this point to keep the lining from rolling to the outside of the garment. (See figure 8.) Instructions for topstitching are on page 143; piping instructions are on page 145.

Figure 8. Understitching

8. Turn the vest right side out by reaching in through one of the open back side seams and pulling both lower fronts out through the same opening (figure 9). Press.

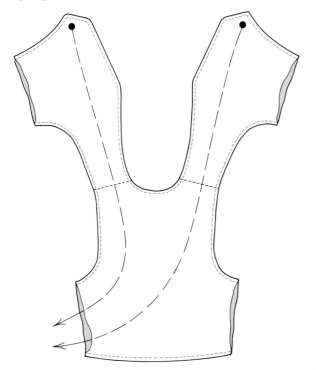

Figure 9. Turning the vest right side out

9. Pin the outer vest together at the side seams, matching the seamlines at the armhole and lower

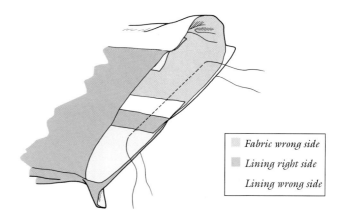

▨	*Fabric wrong side*
▨	*Lining right side*
	Lining wrong side

Figure 10. Stitching the side seams

edge, and keeping the lining free. Stitch, starting about midway along the side, across the vest/lining seam, and ending about 1" (2.5 cm) into the lining. (See figure 10.) Then stitch the same way from the center in the other direction. Backstitch securely at the ends of the seams. Press.

10. Fold the lining seam allowances to the inside along the marked lines; press. Stitch the seams by hand.

11. For button and buttonhole placement, remember that there is an overlap of 1-1/4" (3.2 cm) at the center front.

31

■ Alternate Construction ■

FOR A VEST with bound outer edges, the construction steps are slightly different.

1. Cut the vest and lining as described in the instructions above.

2. Sew the vest fronts to the back at the shoulder seams.

3. Sew the lining fronts to the back at the shoulder seams.

4. With the right sides together, sew the lining to the vest around the armholes. Turn the vest right side out; then trim and press the seams.

5. With *wrong* sides together, sew the vest to the lining around the outer edges. Trim the seam allowance to 1/8" (3 mm).

6. Finish with a braid trim or bias edging as described on page 143.

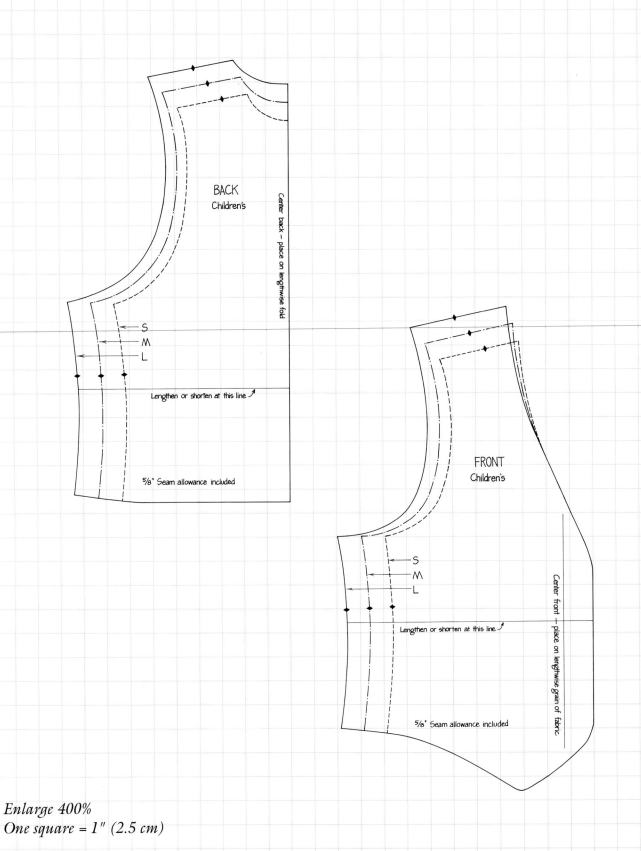

BACK
Children's

Center back – place on lengthwise fold

S
M
L

Lengthen or shorten at this line

⅝" Seam allowance included

FRONT
Children's

Center front – place on lengthwise grain of fabric

S
M
L

Lengthen or shorten at this line

⅝" Seam allowance included

32

Enlarge 400%
One square = 1" (2.5 cm)

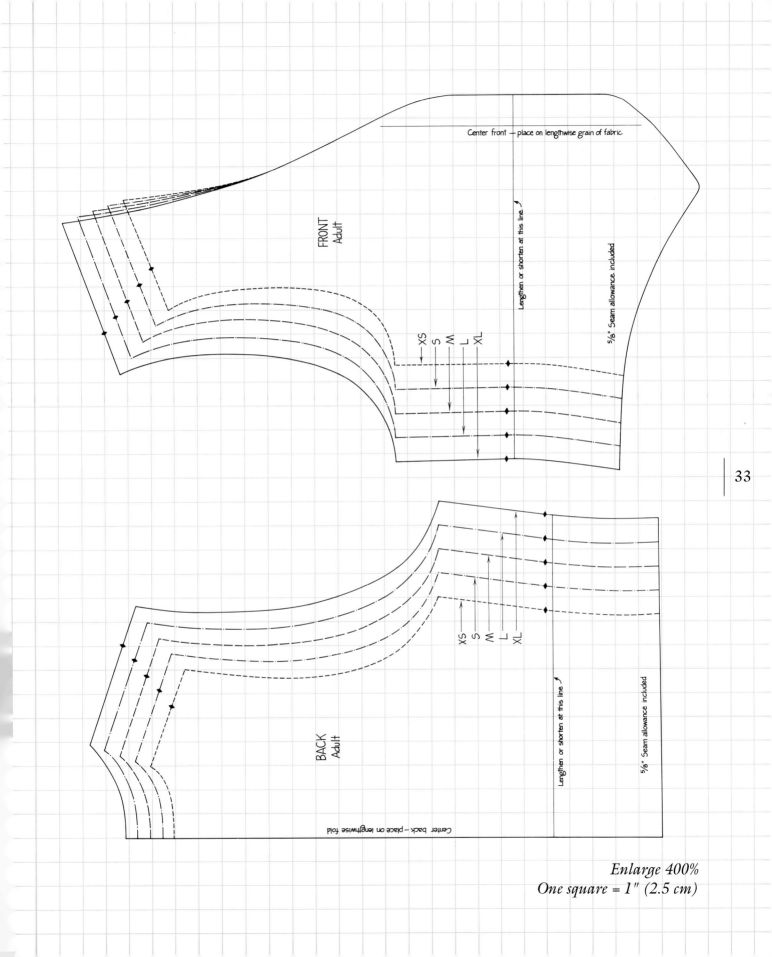

Center front — place on lengthwise grain of fabric.

FRONT
Adult

Lengthen or shorten at this line

⁵⁄₈" Seam allowance included

XS
S
M
L
XL

33

XS
S
M
L
XL

BACK
Adult

Lengthen or shorten at this line

⁵⁄₈" Seam allowance included

Center back — place on lengthwise fold

Enlarge 400%
One square = 1" (2.5 cm)

Sometimes the simplest designs are the most effective. A richly patterned or textured fabric rarely needs further ornamentation. With plain fabric, the addition of just one special element—a single marvelous button, an appliquéd motif, or decorative topstitching—can result in an out-of-the-ordinary garment. The vests in this chapter all are straightforward in their construction, but each designer has added just a little something extra to make the vest unique.

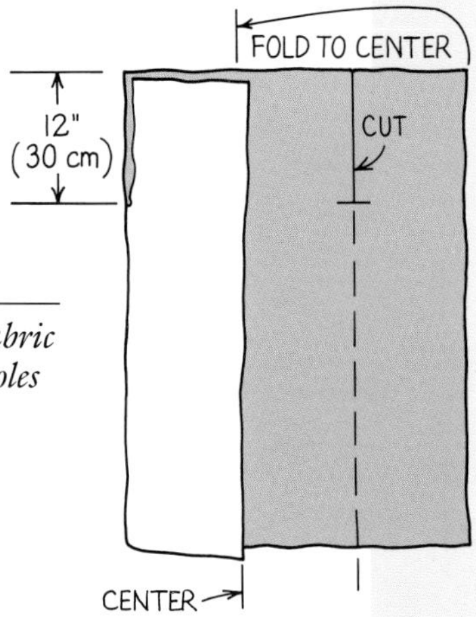

A large square scarf converts easily into a graceful vest, with no pattern necessary! The vest in the photo is sheer rayon chiffon, but any soft, light fabric would work just as well. Fabric can be purchased for the project too; it takes only 1-1/4 yards (1.1 m).

For hems and seams on sheer fabric, a zigzag stitch set at medium length and width will produce a rolled hem or seam. If your machine has adjustable needle positions, you can use the buttonhole foot to guide the rolled edge smoothly. The exact stitch settings you use will depend on the thickness of your fabric. Experiment, if possible, with a scrap or with a fabric of similar weight.

If you use a scarf, leave the hemmed edges intact. With new fabric, trim away the side selvages. Place the scarf or fabric flat on a table and fold in the two sides, lengthwise, to meet at the center. (See figure 1.) Make sure that both sides of are equal width; these will form the front of the vest. To make armholes, cut down along each side fold to a point 12" (30.5 cm) from the top. Cut a small round keyhole at the bottom of each armhole for easier hemming (figure 2); then stitch the hems.

On the upper back, mark off about 7" (17.8 cm) at the center for the neckline. The remainder on either side will form the back shoulders. Gather the top front edges to fit the back shoulders, stitch, and hem all raw edges. (See figure 3.)

Figure 1. Folding the fabric and cutting the armholes

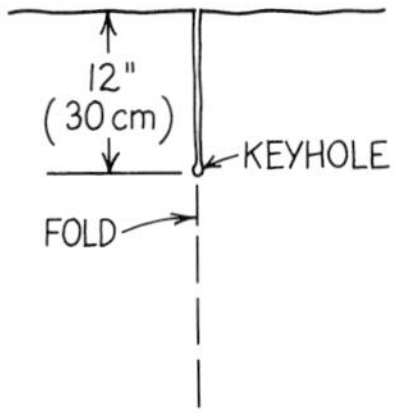

Figure 2. Making a keyhole cut

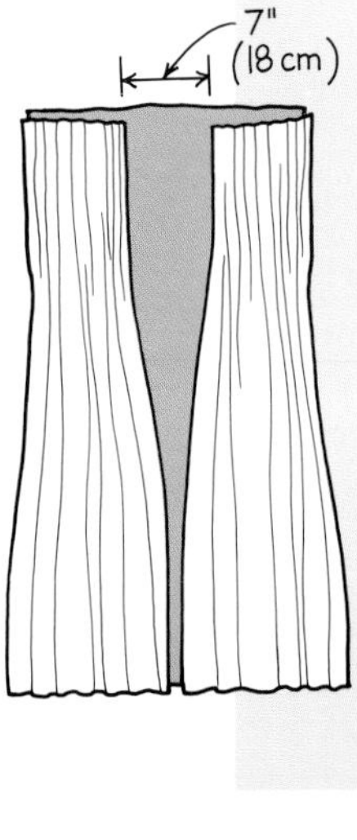

Figure 3. Gathering the top front edges to form the shoulders

DESIGN
Susan Kinney

Clever front pockets customize an otherwise unadorned vest, adding a feature that's essential to this designer's work clothes—she also teaches elementary school. The lining for the vest and pockets is appropriately printed with bright red apples. For complete instructions on adding pockets to your vest, see page 153.

DESIGN
Suzanne Koppi

ermanent fabric marking pens can quickly transform a plain vest into a work of art and provide a few hours of great entertainment at the same time. Make several for kids to decorate at a birthday party; let the office staff sign one for a hospitalized co-worker; reproduce a special picture or a favorite poem; announce the birth of a baby—the potential is unlimited!

A plain purchased vest would serve just as well, but this one has been made from our pattern, using unbleached cotton muslin for both the vest and lining. To add a simple finishing touch, the neck, front, and lower edges are bound with cotton twill tape. The total construction time (after preshrinking the materials) is only about one hour; the cost is minimal if you search out inexpensive muslin from outlet stores.

DESIGN
Rachel Hill

ess than a yard of beautiful fabric and a few well-chosen buttons can turn a simple vest pattern into an elegant wardrobe addition. This patterned rayon velvet is lined with black brocade for a rich combination of textures.

38

DESIGN
Pam Cauble

A delightfully simple design, this vest is proof that the good ideas don't all come from the pros! Dylan Babb, shown here modeling her own vest, is a novice sewer and a dancer as well, and she likes clothes that move.

The pattern has been lengthened somewhat, and cut straight around the lower edge. Lengths of grosgrain ribbon are sewn into the shoulder and neckline seams, then pinked across the free ends to prevent raveling.

DESIGN
Dylan Babb

The multicolored silk tweed in this vest is cleverly accented with triangular shapes that have been cut from lightweight synthetic suede and sewn into the front seams. The vest back is a solid deep purple wool.

Heavier silk fabrics have little "memory," and underlining them with a very light iron-on interfacing, such as the weft-insertion type, helps them retain their shape.

DESIGN
Sherry Masters

The impression it makes is totally glamorous, but the vest beneath the glitter is quite straightforward. Cotton/polyester batiste underlining strengthens the satin fabric used for the vest front. To outline the diamond pattern, gold middy braid is machine stitched onto the front pieces; then the sequins are sewn by hand, each with a matching seed bead to hold it in place. (See page 139 for some tips on attaching sequins.) The back is plain gold satin, without sequins. A decorative gold braid, sewn to the edges of the front, neck, and armholes, completes the design.

DESIGN
Leslie Dierks

The distinctive pattern in this handwoven fabric results from the shifted warp, or Kasuri ikat technique, used in the weaving. The fabric is woven from cotton and wool, and the vest is simply constructed to show off the material. The designer named this one the "Best in the West Vest."

For nonweavers, handwoven fabrics are often readily available in the relatively small quantities needed to make a vest. Check your area craft fairs and galleries for the work of local artists. For some helpful hints on working with handwoven fabrics, see page 150.

DESIGN
Allison Dennis

Sometimes the unlikeliest sources provide inspiration. This design came from the cover illustration on a telephone directory! A basic black vest of silk noil is the backdrop for colorful swirls of rayon ribbon floss, each couched to the vest and accented with a matching button. Additional strands of the floss are sewn into the neckline seam and interwoven, with their ends left to flutter.

Silk noil needs a backing to support the machine stitching this design requires. A firm, lightweight cotton can be sewn to the vest pieces, or a very lightweight fusible interfacing, such as tricot or weft insertion, might be used. Baste or press on the backing; then complete the design work—buttons too— before lining the vest. Couch each ribbon floss strand in place (refer to page 142 for details on couching). Place a dab of liquid fray retardant on the ribbon ends to keep them tidy.

DESIGN
Mary Parker

When a professional artist makes a vest, the logical fabric choice is—what else—artists' canvas! Several washings are required to remove all of the sizing, but the result is a fabric that is soft and wearable. This one has been dyed black, then painted with acrylic paints and fabric paints. Since the acrylics stiffen the fabric somewhat, the artist restricted her designs to small areas. See the section on dyeing and painting fabrics, page 142, for more details.

DESIGN
Jean Wall Penland

Since a vest requires so little fabric, it doesn't seem at all extravagant to make one or two exclusively for holiday wear. This bright Christmas print, garnished with just the right amount of glitter and trim, becomes a very festive vest. The cotton fabric is fairly light in weight, so cotton flannel underlining is used to give it body.

Gold star-shaped sequins of assorted sizes, each topped with a small glass bead, are stitched at random over the front. (See page 139 for hints on attaching sequins and beads.) The gold trim is a purchased welted cord that is sewn into the seam, and the back is snow-white moiré taffeta. A design could hardly be less complicated—or more effective!

DESIGN
Judith Robertson

45

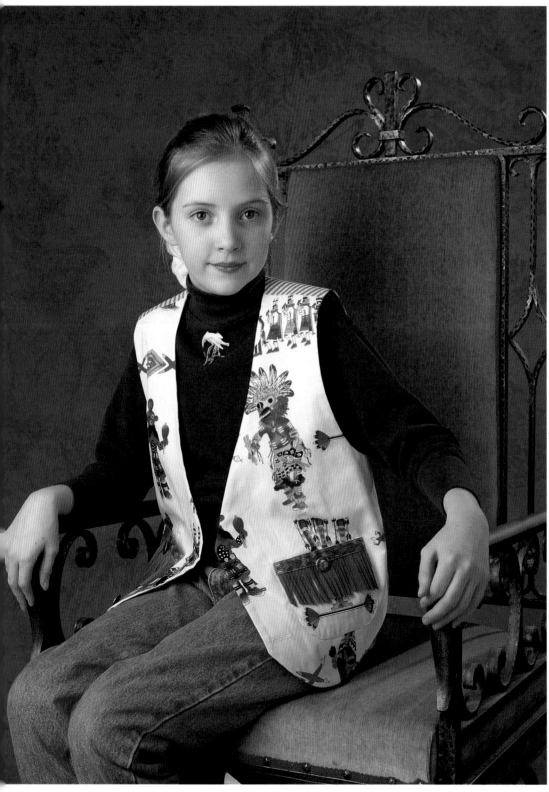

In keeping with the Southwestern theme of the fabric's print, the small patch pockets on this vest are accented with printed ribbon and synthetic suede fringe. (For more pocket ideas, see page 153.) Add a bold striped cotton for the back and lining, and you'll have an entirely different look from the same basic pattern.

DESIGN
Beth Hill

An elegant fabric such as this handwoven silk wants nothing to detract from its beauty. The fabric's unusual pattern results from the shifted warp, or Kasuri ikat, technique used to produce it. Simple lines and good workmanship let the fabric speak for itself. For hints on sewing handwoven fabrics, see page 150.

47

DESIGN
Allison Dennis

E NHANCING A FABRIC BEGINS WITH LOOKING AT A PIECE OF MATERIAL, PERFECTLY LOVELY JUST AS IT IS, AND IMAGINING WHAT MIGHT BE DONE TO MAKE IT EVEN BETTER. DECORATIVE STITCHING EMBELLISHES A RATHER PLAIN FABRIC; A FEW BEADS OR SEQUINS HIGHLIGHT DESIGNS ON A PRINT. FABRICS CAN BE PIECED TOGETHER TO CREATE ENTIRELY NEW FABRICS. APPLIQUÉ CHANGES SHAPES, QUILTING ADDS DIMENSION, AND PLEATING, CRUMPLING, OR COUCHING GIVES THE FABRIC AN ALTOGETHER DIFFERENT TEXTURE. A VEST REQUIRES SUCH A SMALL AMOUNT OF MATERIAL THAT IT'S A PERFECT PLAYGROUND FOR EXPERIMENTING WITH FABRIC MANIPULATION AND EMBELLISHMENT. AFTER SEEING WHAT THESE DESIGNERS HAVE DONE WITH THEIR VESTS, YOU'LL LOOK AT FABRICS IN A WHOLE NEW LIGHT!

C areful design, rich fabrics, and just a touch of decoration produce a very elegant vest. Here motifs and colors are taken from the tapestry and repeated as appliqué or machine-stitched outlines on black silk noil. Metallic fabric and thread, used sparingly, add a dash of sparkle.

To allow a nice balance of the pieced fabrics, the pattern front is cut both vertically and horizontally. The silk noil sections are underlined with very light fusible tricot, giving them the same weight as the tapestry. Because of the rather dense stitching required, a tear-away backing is used behind the appliqué.

Satin stitch borders the appliqué pieces, with a line of straight stitch along each side of the satin stitch to highlight it. Stitching continues to the back and concludes with a sprinkle of stars on one shoulder.

SEWING AIDS, SEE:

Appliqué, page 136
Machine embroidery,
page 147
Piecing and patchwork,
page 150

48

49

D E S I G N
R o b b i e   S p i v e y

SEWING AIDS, SEE:

Appliqué, page 136
Embroidery, page 146
Quilting, page 155
Pattern alterations, page 24

Delicate colors and fresh daffodils: what could be better to herald the arrival of spring? Exquisite appliqué, hand embroidered, echoes the textures and colors of the striped silk background. Quilting along the stripes gives them dimension.

A modest adjustment of the pattern—it is cut slightly lower in the front and squared off at the center—creates lines that work well with the striped fabric. To enhance the quilting, the vest is backed with lightweight polyester fleece.

Lightweight cotton fabrics are used for the appliqué pieces, which are applied using an out-of-the-ordinary technique. The edges are not turned under; instead, they're treated with liquid fray retardant to discourage raveling. A blanket stitch, worked in cotton embroidery floss, covers the raw edges and hides any discoloration caused by the fray retardant. Each daffodil trumpet is accented with a tiny pearl bead.

or an interesting "before-and-after" look, use a single fabric with and without embellishment. Here thick and thin cotton yarns, similar in weight to those woven into the manufactured fabric, are couched in an intricate geometric pattern on one side of the vest, creating an entirely different fabric. (See page 142 for details on couching.)

The fabric, a medium-weight cotton/linen blend, is backed with fusible lightweight weft-insertion interfacing to support the stitching. A perfect button choice and welted cord trim give this vest its crisp, professional-looking finish.

DESIGN
Mary Parker

This vest is easy to make and fun to wear, and it never needs ironing! The technique calls for 100 percent cotton fabric, the more ravel-prone the better. The designer's version is soft, medium-weight chambray, alternated with madras plaid for the ruffles. (Allow an extra yard/.9 meter of fabric for ruffles.) This vest won't develop its full shaggy potential until it has been machine washed and dried at least once.

Construction steps for this vest are a bit different from the basic procedures, and it is unlined. First make some changes to the pattern. Cut the pattern pieces to about 2" (5 cm) shorter than the desired finished length of the vest, and round off the front corners, eliminating the points. (See figure 1 on page 26.) Then cut the vest from the altered pattern.

Stitch the back and fronts together at the sides and shoulders, overcasting the seams to keep them from raveling. Make a double hem around the armholes: Fold the seam allowance to the wrong side and press. Now fold the raw edge in to the first fold, press, and stitch close to the fold.

Measure the outer edge of the vest all the way around. On the cross grain of the extra fabric, cut enough 5" (12.7 cm) strips to equal six times your measurement, plus several inches extra. Fold the strips in half lengthwise, *right side out,* and press the fold. Clip the fabric strips at 1/2" (1.3 cm) intervals, cutting from the raw edges to within 1" (2.5 cm) of the fold. (See figure 1.)

Starting at some point on the back or side of the vest, on the *wrong* side, position a fabric strip with its folded edge extending just beyond the raw edge of the vest. Stitch, using about a 3/8" (1 cm) seam. If the strip doesn't reach all the way around the vest, just start another one right next to the first. When you reach the starting point, cut off the excess strip where the ends meet. Press the seam allowance toward the vest. On the right side, topstitch close to the fold.

Position the next strip on the *right* side of the vest, its folded edge 5/8" (1.6 cm) inside the edge of the first strip so that the cut edge overlaps the stitching on the first strip. Stitch it to the vest, sewing close to the fold. It might be easier first to mark the placement line with a water-soluble fabric marker, then position the strip along the line as you sew. Sew the remaining fabric strips in the same way.

DESIGN
Liz Lima

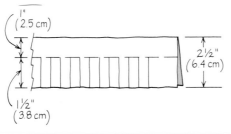

Figure 1. Cutting strips of fringe

From three black and gold cotton prints and an assortment of gold trims, this designer has created a riot of glitter and texture. To make a similar garment, crumple pieces of one or more print fabrics, and fuse them to a backing. Using gold metallic thread, stitch the pleats and wrinkles in place with machine embroidery. Then couch the gold trims with black thread. Finally, join the pieces together with corded gold piping sewn into the seams.

On this vest, golden rosettes decorate one shoulder, and a thick golden rope of stuffed tubing winds over the other. The back is the striped fabric, crumpled and stitched, with a diagonal row of golden buttonholes running from shoulder to hem. A knotted gold ribbon threads through the buttonholes. Lining the vest is the unadorned striped fabric.

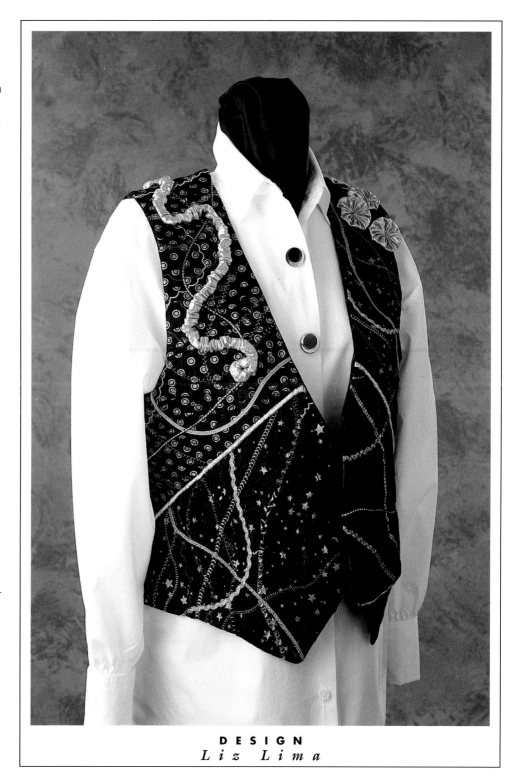

DESIGN
Liz Lima

53

SEWING AIDS, SEE:

Fabric manipulation, page 149
Piecing and patchwork, page 150
Machine embroidery, page 147

Piping, page 145
Couching, page 142

DESIGN
B e t h   H i l l

The full moon, adorned with gold sequins, shines down on a pack of serenading coyotes. A beaded giant saguaro cactus sports red sequined blossoms. Glass beads highlight kernels on the Indian corn and the eyes of coyotes and snakes. This whimsical Southwestern print would make a fine vest all on its own, without further ado. With the addition of quilting, beading, and corded piping trim made of cheerful red cotton flannel, the designer has made it into a masterpiece that's hers alone. The vest's back is the same red flannel used for the piping.

The stuffed quilting, or trapunto, used to highlight the figures is an effective technique for adding a dimensional quality to fabric. It makes selected areas of the design seem to pop out. To support the quilting, polyester fleece underlines the vest front.

SEWING AIDS, SEE:

Beads and sequins, page 139
Trapunto, page 155
Piping, page 145

A few lines of machine quilting and a delicately embroidered iris enhance the water-color pattern of this silk charmeuse without over-whelming it. Areas of color are highlighted with straight stitching, using rayon thread, and with a few wavy stitch lines to add contrast. Small pearl beads give dimension to the flower. For a lining as elegant as the vest itself, the designer chose violet charmeuse. A single abalone shell button and precise edge stitch-ing finish the vest to perfection.

The iris design, repeated on the back, can be drawn on the silk with a water-soluble fabric marker, then stitched free-hand. Very light fusible tricot and thin fleece bat-ting are used behind the soft silk to prevent puck-ered stitching.

SEWING AIDS, SEE:

*Quilting, page 155
Beads and sequins,
page 139*

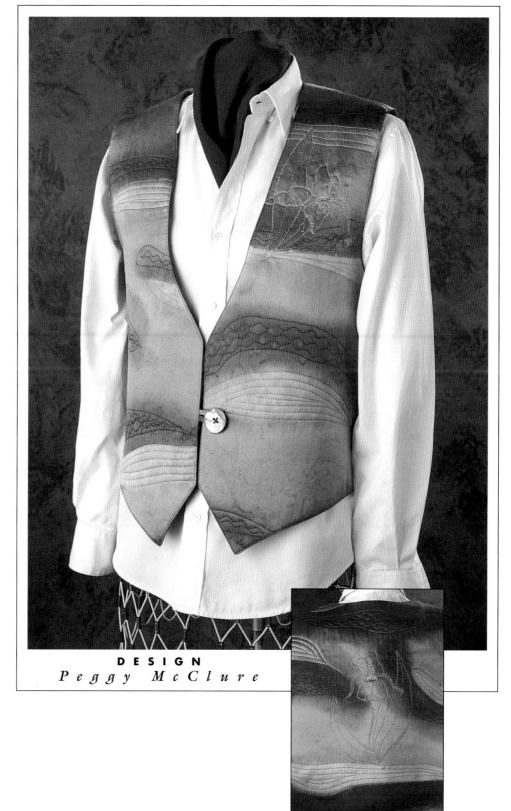

D E S I G N
Peggy McClure

55

DESIGN
Becky Brodersen

C rumpled, pleated, gathered, and pressed, this pretty cotton batik bears little resemblance to the original fabric. The technique is great fun and can produce some surprising results.

In this example, the designer has tucked small pieces of fabric, in assorted colors and patterns, into some of the pleats before stitching them in place. Button loops are stuffed tubes, sewn into the front vest/lining seam. The designer added her "signature"—a leaf motif cut from the fabric (before enhancement) and appliquéd to the lining at the back neckline.

SEWING AIDS, SEE:

*Fabric manipulation,
page 149
Buttons and buttonholes,
page 139*

A well-planned combination of prints—in this case a linen/cotton blend on the front and cotton for the back and lining—is all it takes to make a good-looking vest. But this designer has gone a step further, adding a richly embroidered appliqué to create a sensational work of art.

The appliqué motifs incorporate several complementary prints, rayon thread in all colors, and a wide variety of stitches. Some motifs are applied with rows and rows of straight stitch, some with satin stitch, and some using decorative machine stitches. For a design of this kind, a certain amount of planning is necessary—size, shape, and arrangement of the motifs—but it's also a wonderful occasion just to let go, stitch away, and watch a fabulous design emerge!

SEWING AIDS, SEE:

Appliqué, page 136
Machine embroidery,
page 147

DESIGN
Lori Kerr

Striped fabrics inspire all sorts of creative designs. These two vests employ the same technique, yet are very different in finished form. Experimentation is the secret!

Firmly woven 100 percent cotton fabric works best because it creases easily and neatly. The fabric used for these vests is stable enough that no backing is needed, but with a lighter weight fabric, or one that has a tendency to stretch, a backing is recommended. For the backing, use a firm, lightweight fabric, such as cotton lawn or batiste, and attach it after pleating.

On the right side, fold and press a tuck along one of the stripes; stitch. Make subsequent tucks by folding and stitching at the same point on each pattern stripe. Press the tucks in one direction, then in the other to reveal the stripes beneath. Then stitch across the tucks to hold them in the desired position.

The lighter colored vest is lined with beige cotton,

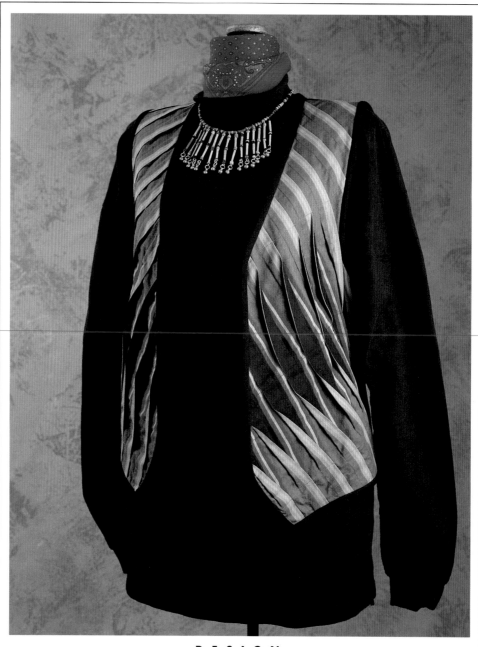

DESIGN
Becky Brodersen

and its edges are bound with bias fabric. The dark vest is edged with bias strips of the same black cotton twill used for the vest back. (Refer to page 144 for tips on making bias edge binding.)

This technique can be as uncomplicated or as intricate as you wish to make it. With finely striped fabric and more tucks, with machine embroidery stitches used to sew the tucks in place, or with decorative threads used for the stitching, a totally different vest would result.

59

Certain vests come into being not because the wardrobe requires another garment, but because a creative person needs to express an idea or experiment with a new technique. A vest, with its relatively small surface area, provides a perfect backdrop for such expression and play. The result is a fabulous addition to the wardrobe.

60

The smallest detail can often spark the best idea! This one began with the miniature Peruvian weaving on the left front of the vest. Beautifully worked satin stitch embroidery, in all sorts of colors and stitch patterns, serves as the unifying element for the great variety of fabrics, shapes, colors, and textures. Seminole patchwork, Latin American color combinations, and ikat-woven fabrics add a multi-cultural aspect as well.

The back of the vest, made of black taffeta, features the designer's hallmark. A design element from the vest's front—a small Seminole square tilted at an angle and bordered with colorful satin stitch—is repeated on one shoulder.

SEWING AIDS, SEE:

Appliqué, page 136
Piecing and patchwork,
page 150
Machine embroidery,
page 147

61

row satin stitch. Handworked French knots form each flower's center.

The twining gold "cord" is actually a line of satin stitch sewn with a metallic thread on top and invisible nylon in the bobbin. The variations in width of the cord are achieved by changing stitch width while sewing. It's a skill not unlike rubbing the head and patting the stomach simultaneously: simple once mastered. Not all machines perform this maneuver, however; before trying it, check the instruction book for your machine to avoid breaking a needle.

DESIGN
Beverly Dawson & Lynda Sanders

An elegant arrangement of silk poppies and leaves is very striking against a background of ivory linen-weave silk. Fine gold cord winds among the flowers to give the design just a hint of glitter.

Light fusible tricot backs the silk to prevent it from stretching out of shape, and tear-away backing is used behind the appliqué and embroidery. Before the motifs are cut, the fabrics used for the appliqués are fused to a paper-backed web. The motifs are then pressed onto the vest and edged with a nar-

SEWING AIDS, SEE:

Appliqué, page 136
Machine embroidery, page 147

Two shades of soft sand-washed linen make a subtle backdrop for an uncomplicated, yet distinctive, appliqué design. Fuse paper-backed web to the fabric to be used for the appliqués—in this case, a plaid—then cut the appliqué motifs from the bonded fabric and apply them to the vest. Because the bonding agent also retards fraying, the edges of the motifs need not be turned under. Instead, stitch around the shapes in a carefree fashion using straight stitch and decorative rayon thread. Highlight the seam joining the two background fabrics with additional decorative stitching as desired.

SEWING AIDS, SEE:

Appliqué, page 136
Piecing and patchwork,
page 150
Machine embroidery,
page 147

DESIGN
Lori Kerr

63

Black appliqué on a boldly colored fabric makes a striking design, yet one that's not at all difficult to execute. The designer's inspiration came from watching hummingbirds sip nectar from the morning glories outside her window on summer mornings. She traced shapes from illustrations in nature guidebooks, then cut several of each from paper to plan their arrangement on the vest.

The motifs are lightweight synthetic suede. Since the fabric doesn't ravel, the shapes can be sewn in place, close to the edges, with machine straight stitching. The flowers and leaves grow on vines of embroidery floss that's held in place with couching. Sew-in polyester fleece, very light in weight, underlines the silk noil background fabric.

SEWING AIDS, SEE:

Appliqué, page 136
Couching, page 142

DESIGN
Mary Parker

uted colors and soft fabrics enhance this vest's woodsy feel. Oak leaves and acorns, made of silk and wool, are applied to a silk noil background, then detailed with meticulous hand embroidery. "It's best to use no more than three to five different stitches on a garment," the designer suggests. Hand-worked button-holes and old pearl buttons add a very elegant touch. For comfort, the vest is lined with soft green wool flannel.

To allow for a continuous design such as this one, cut the pattern without side seams, and attach the lining before sewing the shoulder seams. Be sure to include an underlining—cotton organdy is used here—to add body to the silk and to provide support for the appliqué work.

SEWING AIDS, SEE:

Appliqué, page 136
Embroidery, page 146

D E S I G N
R o b b i e   S p i v e y

DESIGN
Cathy Carlson

The designer, the granddaughter of Norwegian immigrants, was taught that country's traditional embroidery as a child. In the stunning designs on her black wool vest she uses traditional materials and hand embroidery stitches, creating variations of the old patterns. The design on the front was inspired by the rose embroidery of Norway's Telemark region. The predominant stitches are stem and satin stitch, worked in Norwegian wool yarns and cotton floss. (Refer to page 146 for instructions on embroidery stitches.)

On the back, she has rendered her own interpretation of the traditional patterns with a spiral design representative of reindeer antlers and the spirit of the Norwegian countryside. The inner stitches of the spiral are free of the fabric, but the outer edges are connected with couching, chain, and stem stitches. Two important images, the wolf and the mountain goat, are meticulously stitched using a single strand of floss.

This jewel of a vest features shimmery satin patches in gemstone colors, all richly outlined with hand embroidery. Thread colors are chosen for contrast with the background colors to give wonderful clarity to the stitches. French knots and a variety of other stitches—daisy, running stitch, satin, feather, cretan, and cross stitch— are all represented here, together with quite a few combinations besides! In addition to cotton floss, silk and rayon threads are used to add more variety to the stitches. Black satin for the vest's back and lining serves to emphasize its colorful character.

SEWING AIDS, SEE:

Piecing and patchwork,
page 150
Embroidery, page 146

DESIGN
Nancy Granner

DESIGN
Mary Parker

*S*ashiko is a traditional Japanese embroidery technique that features gridded patterns worked in running stitch on indigo-dyed fabrics.

Here is an interpretation of the technique for the sewing machine, using heavy cotton topstitching thread in the bobbin and stitching on the back of the fabric. (Refer to page 147 for more information on machine embroidery.)

The fabric used for this vest is dark blue silk noil, with a backing of lightweight polyester batting. As with any machine embroidery, the pieces should be cut larger than the pattern initially, then cut to size after the stitching has been completed.

Trace the designs onto soft, nonwoven gridded pattern-drafting material that you've basted onto the batting. Then stitch directly over the pencil lines. The trick, according to the designer, is to plan the sewing direction for the longest possible line of continuous stitching (which means fewer threads to knot later) and to avoid stitching any line twice.

Intricate metallic thread stitchery elevates this vest from merely wonderful to very glamorous indeed. The designer has added lots of texture: The patchwork incorporates a great variety of fabrics, and the freeform stitching and topstitching are worked with all sorts of decorative stitches and threads. Soft black brocade is used for the back of the vest, and violet satin makes the lining.

Crazy-quilt patchwork makes a great background for stitch experimentation. Mistakes are almost impossible, and innovations in stitch techniques are almost guaranteed!

SEWING AIDS, SEE:

Couching, page 142
Machine embroidery,
page 147
Piecing and patchwork,
page 150

D E S I G N
L o r i   K e r r

P erhaps a sort of primal scream therapy for sewers, this is an "anything goes" quilting technique that produces a most distinctive garment! Pure cotton fabrics work best, with bits of other natural fiber fabrics used for accent if desired. The fronts and back can be solid pieces of a single fabric, like the vest shown, or they can be pieced together to incorporate any number of patterns and fabrics. The outer edges and armholes are bound with small squares of folded fabric in any combination. Edges of the squares are left unfinished, and after a few trips through the washer and dryer, they will fluff up nicely, ravel a bit, and contribute a special shaggy quality to the look of the vest. The finished product is automatically reversible.

To make the vest, cut fabric for the front and back, and for the "lining" front and back, leaving an extra inch or so (a few centimeters) at all the outer edges. If you're piecing your fabrics, do the piecing before cutting from the pattern. Cut a backing—cotton flannel is good—and pin it to the outer vest pieces.

Sew the outer vest together at the shoulder and side seams, with the right sides together. Do the same for the inner vest. Now put the inner and outer vest together, right sides out, and baste loosely around the edges.

For the edge bindings, cut 3" (7.6 cm) squares of fabric (any pattern combination) from the straight grain of the fabric. How many? Many!

Now the fun begins. Quilt the vest together, starting somewhere in the center and working toward the outer edges. Use a straight stitch and work in a zigzag pattern: a few inches (several centimeters) forward, then a similar distance in reverse at a slightly different angle. Stitching should be equally dense over the entire surface, but beyond that it's your choice. Change thread colors (no need to worry about tying the ends); use a decorative thread here and there; throw in an embroidery stitch now and then. For accent, small squares of contrasting fabric can be applied while quilting to repeat the edge design. On the vest shown, a row of angled overlapping squares is sewn down the center back.

When the quilting is finished, use the pattern to trim the outer edges and armhole edges, eliminating seam allowances and the center front overlap. To bind the raw edges, fold one of the small squares, previously cut for this purpose, in half *diagonally* over an edge, and stitch it in place on the vest, stitching as you did for the quilting. Fold the next square over the edge, slightly overlapping the first, and stitch it. Continue all the way around, binding the outer edge and the armholes in the same way. The bias edges of the folded squares will conform to the curved edges of the vest.

SEWING AIDS, SEE:

Piecing and patchwork,
page 150
Quilting, page 155

70

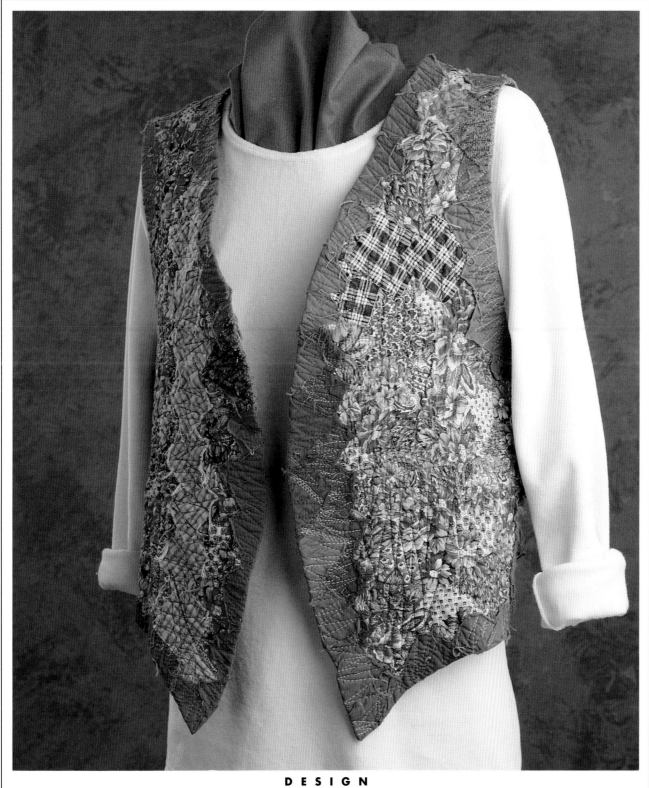

71

DESIGN
Created by Liz Lima,
based on a technique developed by Bird Ross

DESIGN
Susan Kinney

This designer employs an unusual technique for fabric patterning. The fabric—a simple, unbleached cotton muslin—is dyed black, and chlorine bleach is used to remove color from the design areas, in this case X's and O's (for kisses and hugs?). Sound like fun? For accents the designer added random French knots of brightly colored yarn. The buttons are made of polymer clay, a modeling compound, to duplicate the shapes of the design motifs. A bright yarn loop fastens them together. (See page 139 for more ideas on adding buttons and buttonholes.)

Prewash the fabric and dye it. Use a good commercial fabric dye, available from craft supply stores, and follow the manufacturer's directions carefully. When the fabric is dry, cut the vest pieces.

In a sink or large bucket, prepare a neutralizing bath by adding one part vinegar to 16 parts water. Find a work surface that's impervious to bleach, cover it thickly with newspapers, and lay out the vest pieces. Then pour a small amount of bleach into a glass cup. Using an *old* paintbrush (the bleach will eat the bristles), paint designs onto the fabric. A little practice beforehand with your fabric scraps will help you get the feel of the technique. Work quickly, and rinse each piece in the neutralizing solution as soon as the design work is finished. Then rinse thoroughly in plain water to remove the vinegar smell.

The combination of wine-colored linen, printed cotton, and green silk noil creates a rich blend of both colors and textures. Inside, a decadently soft lining of tan washed silk begs to be touched. Outside, the designer has applied her colors skillfully. Dark green is chosen for the accents. It's used for the thin crossed strips applied to the front, the thread color for quilting and embroidery, and for the buttonholes.

To lengthen the vest and exaggerate its style, as shown here, the pattern is cut horizontally at the chest line. For piecing, this vest has a cut made approximately parallel to the front edge, and a V-shaped cut at the center back.

SEWING AIDS, SEE:

Appliqué, page 136
Pattern alterations, page 24
Piecing and patchwork,
page 150
Quilting, page 155
Machine embroidery,
page 147

DESIGN
Lori Kerr

74

Blending colors and patterns of a dozen assorted fabrics into a single exquisite garment takes a practiced eye and plenty of time. Here the patchwork is scaled down to proportions that are suited to a vest. Pieced fabric "stripes" of varying widths are interspersed with strips of patchwork in a flattering diagonal pattern on the front of the vest and in a vertical design on the back. Intricate machine quilting, stitched in two colors, covers the entire vest. The stitching is done freehand fashion, creating its own wonderful patterns of swirls and curlicues.

The vest is reversible. On the inside is a single fabric, and for accents, the shoulder and side seams are bound with the same bias-cut fabric that binds the outer edges. A light batting—cotton flannel works well—is used between the layers.

This vest requires a construction sequence that is slightly different from the standard. Piecing is done first; then, to allow for a bit of shrinkage from the quilting, all of the vest pieces are cut out slightly larger than the pattern. Sandwich the fabric layers for each vest component and quilt them together. Then recut each piece by the pattern after quilting. With "right" sides together, join the shoulder and side seams.

For binding the seam allowances, cut a bias strip of fabric about 1-1/4" (about 3 cm) wide and as long as the seam. Place the strip along the seam allowance with the edge of the strip in the seam allowance, about 1/4" (6 mm) from the seamline. Stitch on the seamline. Press toward the seam allowance, then over the edges of the seam allowance. Press the seam allowances down, covering the raw edge of the bias strip. Then stitch the folded edge in place by machine or by hand. Similarly, bind the front edges and armholes with bias strips.

The clever buttonholes used here work from either side of the vest. Just incorporate narrow bias tubes into the binding seam at the front edge so that they flip over the binding to button and lie neatly out of the way when they're not in use.

SEWING AIDS, SEE:

Piecing and patchwork,
page 150
Quilting, page 155
Bias edge binding, page 144
Buttons and buttonholes,
page 139

DESIGN
Karen James Swing

In the back of every closet lurks a garment that hasn't been worn for years, yet is always exempted from the annual closet clean-out. Perhaps it has sentimental value, or it's made of exceptional fabric. Perhaps it should be recycled into a vest!

The lucky among us have treasures from great aunts or grandmothers—doilies, dresser scarves, or linen guest towels that are trimmed with some beautiful, time-consuming form of needlework that we ourselves will never undertake. Maybe you have a collection of old pearl buttons, military medals, or scout badges somewhere. These too have great vest-making potential.

If annual moves or a fussy spouse have prevented your building a stockpile, there are flea markets, antique stores, consignment shops, and dozens of other sources for vintage raw materials.

The collection of vests in this chapter demonstrates a variety of ways to get treasured fabrics—and other materials—out of their hiding places and into your active wardrobe.

The soft cotton challis fabric of a favorite old dress inspired this designer to recycle. To give the vest a new element all its own, she appliquéd a graceful willow tree on the back. The tree shape was cut from green silk noil, then applied with hand-worked blanket stitch. The tree's branches and leaves are embroidered in chain stitch with silk cord to add luster and texture to the appliqué.

SEWING AIDS, SEE:

Appliqué, page 136
Embroidery, page 146
Pattern alterations, page 24

DESIGN
Robbie Spivey

DESIGN
Mary Parker

tons. The back and the corded piping trim are solid-colored taffeta.

This vest requires careful planning, though its assembly is not at all difficult. It's layered from the bottom up, with the lower edge of each layer left free (similar to fish scales). Each layer, except the one at the bottom of the vest, is doubled fabric, making a self facing.

Plan the arrangement of fabrics on a copy of the pattern as you would for any pieced vest. All layers extend all of the way across one front piece and are sewn into the side and center front seams. Each layer should extend upward far enough to provide a background wherever you want to have a window in the layer above it. Cut two fronts from lightweight fabric to use as backings for your assemblies.

Where a window is planned, locating it as far as possible from the lower edge of its layer makes for easier construction. To sew a window, place the fabric layer and its facing with

Seldom-worn formal clothing can often provide interesting fabrics for vests. Here pieces of tapestry fabric and iridescent taffeta are layered in a very intriguing manner for a most unusual effect. Small round windows give a glimpse of the layers below and frame three heirloom but-right sides together. Trace a circle for the window, and stitch around it with a fairly short stitch. Cut away the fabric inside the circle, trimming and clipping close to the stitching. Turn the window right side out by pulling one layer through the other; press. To sew the lower edge seam, don't pull the facing back through the window, but turn the fabrics just at the edges so that the right sides are together. Align the edges; then stitch a little of the seam at a time, using a narrow seam allowance. Press the seam.

Attach each layer to the backing, sewing close to the upper raw edges of the layer. Baste the layers in place at the outer edges and armholes, and finish the vest in the standard way.

SEWING AIDS, SEE:

Piecing and patchwork, page 150
Piping, page 145

DESIGN
Jennifer Thomas

Accompanied by a photograph and a story or two, this silk noil vest makes a very special gift for a young girl.

Her great-grandmother's pearl buttons and crochet work provide the embellishments, together with new ribbon bows and couched rayon cord for lustrous accents. It's underlined with cotton flannel, a fabric that works especially well with silk noil and feels comfortable to wear.

The fabric, a souvenir of a memorable vacation in Guatemala, was originally made into a skirt that was not particularly flattering. The skirt was soon relegated to the attic, but the fabric still had potential. There was plenty of material for a vest, and rearranging the stripes provided lots of design interest. The narrow diagonal pieces across the front are bias strips, folded in half and sewn into the seam that joins the upper and lower sections, then pressed flat. Dyed horn beads serve as buttons, with linen cord loops for buttonholes.

DESIGN
the author

SEWING AIDS, SEE:

*Piecing and patchwork,
page 150
Buttons and buttonholes,
page 139*

*An unflattering skirt
can make a great vest.*

A favorite 1930s rayon dress (one that had seen lots of parties in the 1980s), a companionable vintage bathrobe found in a local thrift shop, and a single silk necktie provided the fabric for an almost-traditional vest. To provide a piecing seam and to add shaping, the pattern front is cut on a curve from the armhole to the lower edge. (For more on pattern alterations, see page 24.) Small front pockets, fabric to cover the buttons, and a tie belt for the back are all cut from the one necktie. The vest's back and lining are navy rayon.

DESIGN
Dana Irwin

T he gift of a bagful of necktie salesmen's old silk samples proved a vest maker's dream come true! In this design, the scraps are pieced into lengthwise strips and stitched to a muslin backing, working from the center fronts toward the sides of the vest. (See page 150 for more information on this technique.) A muted, navy cotton print lines the vest, and the back is navy tropical-weight wool.

For those not lucky enough to have access to such treasures, old silk neckties from flea markets and the like would also serve. One caveat: fabric gleaned from ties is cut on the bias and must have a backing to prevent unsightly stretching. A very lightweight fusible weft-insertion or tricot interfacing serves the purpose nicely.

82

DESIGN
Pat Taylor

The color pink provides the common element in a display of old embroidered linens and crocheted doilies. All are arranged on a background of white cotton damask, also used for the vest's back. (For more information about piecing fabrics, see page 150.) Pearl buttons accentuate the curved edge of one linen piece and add interest to the crochet. The lining is a very appropriate pink and green cotton calico print.

The vest features a creative method for gathering in fullness across the back waist. Vertical machine-made buttonholes are worked at 1" (2.5 cm) intervals all the way across. Pink ribbons are sewn into the side seams, then threaded through the buttonholes and tied at the center.

DESIGN
Pat Moore

83

A long, sheer scarf that no longer complements anything in the wardrobe (or a lucky find in a thrift shop) can produce a very exotic vest in very little time. This one is embroidered silk chiffon, edged with a decorative rayon cord in the same color.

The vest can be made from the basic pattern, with seams only at the shoulders. Tape the front and back pattern pieces together at the side seamlines. There will be a small gap, but don't worry about it.

Fold the scarf in half crosswise. Then place the center back of the pattern on the fold, and cut the vest as one piece. Round off the front points slightly to make hemming easier.

Using a zigzag stitch set at a medium width and a fairly short length, sew the shoulder seams. For hems, lengthen the stitch slightly, and a rolled hem will result. If your machine's needle position is adjustable, use the buttonhole foot to

DESIGN
Susan Kinney

help make the rolled edge neat and even.

Because most of the raw edges are on the fabric's bias, they may ripple somewhat when hemmed this way. If you consider that condition a problem rather than a design feature, simply incorporate a piece of firm, thin cord into the hem as it's sewn. Cut the cord to the pattern; then ease the fabric to fit it while you're rolling the edge. Decorative cord can be applied the same way.

A magnificent tapestry dresser scarf, gracefully aged, becomes the front of an elegant vest for holiday wear. Judiciously placed small beads highlight the woven design. (See page 139 for more details on attaching beads and sequins.) The scarf's attractive border design is left intact at the front and bottom edges of the vest, requiring some adjustment to the pattern. The back of the vest is black velvet, and the lining is antique gold satin.

DESIGN
Robbie Spivey

When a birch tree in her yard succumbed to whatever kills birch trees, this designer looked for a way to preserve its beautiful bark as a garment. She began with a vest made years ago and no longer worn, then sculpted a unique removable collar from the bark. Take note: Living birch trees do not take kindly to having their bark recycled!

To make a collar pattern, tape the front and back vest pattern pieces together at the shoulder, matching seamlines. Draw the desired collar shape, eliminating the front and neck seam allowances. (See figure 3 on page 27.)

In addition to the materials for the basic vest, you will need approximately 1/2 yard (46 cm) of firm interfacing, 2 yards (1.8 m) of 5/8" (1.6 cm) grosgrain ribbon, 1 yard (.9 m) of hook-and-loop fastener, a hot glue gun, and—of course—your birch bark.

Trace the collar shape onto firm interfacing material (or use a double thickness of medium-weight material), and cut. If fusible interfacing is used, fuse the layers together. For sew-in interfacing, stitch the layers together around all the edges and across the interior with a zigzag pattern.

After making a basic lined vest, topstitch the front and neckline about 1" (2.5 cm) from the edge. This will prevent the collar attachments from pulling the lining to the outside. In her vest, the designer used several rows of topstitching around all of the edges for a finish that is both decorative and practical.

Cut pieces of ribbon about 3-1/2" (9 cm) long, and position them along the neck edge of the collar at evenly spaced intervals so that they extend into the neckline at right angles. Stitch them to the underside of the collar. Now stitch a small piece of the *hook* section of the hook-and-loop tape to the underside of each ribbon tab.

With the vest on the body or on a dress form, position the collar on the vest, fold the ribbon tabs over the edge of the vest to the inside, and mark their positions on the inside of the vest. Sew a piece of the *loop* section of the hook-and-loop tape to correspond to each tab.

Now decorate the collar. Glue the birch bark to the collar in small sections to make sure it covers the collar form completely.

DESIGN
Joyce Baldwin

A VEST, LIKE ANY OTHER WORK OF ART, CAN COMMUNICATE A THOUGHT OR SHARE AN IDEA. IT CAN SERVE AS A VISUAL EXPRESSION OF A STORY, POEM, OR MUSICAL THEME. A VEST CAN COMMENT ON A CURRENT EVENT, OR IT CAN PRESERVE ONE OF LIFE'S MEMORABLE EXPERIENCES. PERHAPS THE DESIGNS IN THIS CHAPTER WILL INSPIRE YOU TO RECREATE YOUR OWN THEME AS A VEST.

Her sewing ability is a legacy from her grandmother and great-grandmother, and it seemed appropriate to this designer to display treasured bits of their needlework on a delicate linen vest. Hatpin lace, made in the 1890s, edges the front. A decorative panel on one side includes strips of tatting and antique buttons. At the shoulder is a miniature purse, made by her grandmother to carry a dime for the streetcar when she went on a date, just in case…. The long strap of the purse extends over the shoulder to drape gracefully across the back neckline. (See page 136 for more details on appliqué.)

Linen has an ageless quality that makes it a perfect fabric for displaying heirloom needlework or for creating a modern facsimile. If your own laces are not as antique looking as you would like, you can age them by dyeing them in strong tea.

DESIGN
Beth Hill

After she married an architect, this designer began to view buildings with a more insightful eye. The design for the back of her vest was inspired by a drawing of an eleventh century abbey, its curves and shapes perfect candidates for appliqué. The appliqué pieces are silk, layered in colors chosen to create the illusion of depth and perspective. For an elegant finish, all of the appliqué pieces are edged in satin stitch. The front of the vest is an ikat-weave silk that incorporates the appliqué colors. (For more details on sewing appliqué, refer to page 136.)

DESIGN
Sherry Masters

When she was given her great-grandmother's button collection, this designer created a vest that displays the buttons—and also provides an occasion to share anecdotes of family history with interested admirers. The checked background provides each button its own shadowbox for display. To give the vest a crisp, professional look, it's trimmed with rayon welted cord.

The checked pattern is created from black and white suit-weight silk, assembled using the Seminole patchwork technique. This stretchy silk is best fused to a light weft-insertion or tricot interfacing before the pieces are cut. An additional underlining of firm, lightweight cotton also helps support the weight of the buttons. Because the seamlines are later covered with middy braid, the pieces can be sewn together on the right side of the fabric, their edges abutted, with a bridging or zigzag stitch. The buttons are sewn in place before the vest is lined.

DESIGN
Mary Parker

SEWING AIDS, SEE:

Piecing and patchwork,
page 150
Piping, page 145

When her 27-year marriage ended in divorce, this designer sought to preserve the happy memories to pass along to her daughter. Her medium is not painting or poetry, but patchwork, and she chose a vest to tell the story.

The vest is pieced in strips, incorporating fabrics, laces, and buttons from her wedding dress, along with scraps from trousseau garments. Hand-crocheted medallions denote the years of the marriage, each with a small embroidered symbol of the year's highlight. On the back, a stylized bride and groom are appliquéd and elaborately embroidered by hand.

DESIGN
Robbie Spivey

SEWING AIDS, SEE:

Piecing and patchwork,
page 150
Appliqué, page 136
Embroidery, page 146

hildhood memories of daily life in a large urban center inspired this vest. A picture of city apartment buildings, with laundry drying on clotheslines stretched between them, is whimsically interpreted in rich fabrics and textures. Tiny vests are hung by miniature clothespins from an elastic clothesline that also forms the closure for the vest. Brocade buildings, sporting synthetic suede windows and outlined in beadwork, are appliquéd to a background of cotton velvet. The lining is multicolored striped silk.

93

SEWING AIDS, SEE:

Appliqué, page 136
Beads and sequins,
page 139

DESIGN
N i e s s a   B a u d e r   G u a r a c h a

DESIGN
R o b b i e   S p i v e y

As a gift to her daughter, the designer created a biography in stitches, a vest that recalls special times in her daughter's early life. Crazy patches are adorned with embroidered ballet slippers from dancing school days, the gold cross she wore as a baby, and stitched interpretations of the exotic birds she drew as a child. The vest incorporates the daughter's favorite autumn colors, and it exhibits her mother's skillful hand embroidery.

Here is a note to other vest makers who wonder whether such gifts are appreciated: It was with great reluctance that the vest's recipient agreed to part with her treasure long enough for it to be photographed.

SEWING AIDS, SEE:

*Appliqué, page 136
Piecing and patchwork,
page 150
Embroidery, page 146*

A poem from *Women Who Run with the Wolves* made a lasting impression on this designer. Her interpretation—in vest form—employs triangular patchwork, a favored technique for the color blending it allows. The woman who lives under the lake, the poem's subject, is worked in appliqué. Her "hair of twig" and "dress of weed" are embroidered by machine using rayon threads. Dividing the patchwork sections is an appliquéd border of watery-colored teal, satin stitched in tones of the same color. The vest's back and lining are teal taffeta. Along one back shoulder are a few machine-embroidered leaves to restate the front design.

SEWING AIDS, SEE:

Appliqué, page 136
Piecing and patchwork,
page 150
Machine embroidery,
page 147

95

DESIGN
J i m m i e   B e n e d i c t

DESIGN
the author

If you have a musician in the family, or as a good friend, consider making a customized vest that displays his favorite tune and perhaps serves as a memory aid as well. This one is worked in linen, for greater comfort during summer performances. The staff lines are drawn with machine stitching, and the notes are filled in with a permanent fabric marker. Assorted pockets in the blue chambray lining hold the musician's essential accouterments.

To make your own, plan the layout first on a copy of the pattern. With a fabric such as linen, use a lightweight nonwoven interfacing to counteract its tendency to stretch. Draw the staff lines onto the fabric with powdered chalk marker; then stitch through both layers to hold them together. With any sort of decorative work, it's easiest to do the drawing or painting on the separate pieces before assembling the vest. (See page 142 for more details on painting on fabric.)

oncern for the rain forest ecology led this designer to decorate a silk noil vest with colorful South American frogs, all displaying very froglike postures. Each appliqué, cut from synthetic suede, is held in place with a drop of fabric glue, then zigzag stitched around the edges. The frogs are embellished with machine embroidery, worked in rayon thread, and finished with small button eyes.

DESIGN
Mary Parker

SEWING AIDS, SEE:

Appliqué, page 136
Machine embroidery,
page 147

W hen you're an avid backgammon player, the best stories are told in the process of playing the game! This cleverly designed vest converts quickly to a board: the vest snaps apart to make a flat playing surface, and the playing pieces are kept handy in a pouch suspended from the detachable belt. It has a background fabric of synthetic leather and appliquéd points made of synthetic suede. Strips of the suede fabric also are used to bind the edges. The buttons on the front are made of polymer clay (a modeling compound) to match the playing pieces.

To create an almost rectangular back, a separate underarm pattern piece is needed. The seamlines of the side pieces are extensions of the armhole lines. On the front, the armhole binding extends down to cover the side/front seamline. Only the side/front seams are sewn; the back is fastened to the sides and at the shoulders with hooks and eyes.

SEWING AIDS, SEE:

Pattern alterations, page 24
Appliqué, page 136
Buttons and buttonholes,
page 139

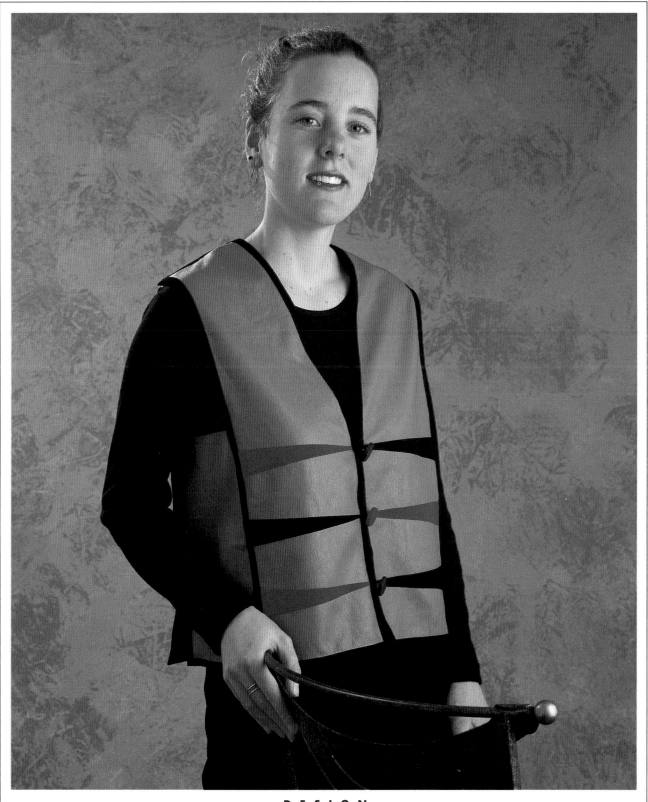

99

DESIGN
Joyce Baldwin

LET THE FABRIC DESIGN THE VEST

SOMETIMES A FABRIC ALMOST TELLS YOU WHAT IT WOULD LIKE TO BECOME. YOU MAY HAVE NO CREATIVE IDEAS AT ALL UNTIL YOU SEE THE FABRIC. A DESIGN SUDDENLY SPRINGS TO LIFE IN YOUR HEAD, COMPLETE DOWN TO THE BUTTONS AND THREAD COLOR. VESTS IN THIS SECTION SHOW HOW WELL DESIGNERS CAN EMPATHIZE WITH THE PERSONALITIES OF THEIR MATERIALS, TAKING FULL ADVANTAGE OF THE FABRICS' CHARACTERISTICS.

Rayon lends itself especially well to fabric manipulation techniques. Here two rayon prints demonstrate how your choice of fabric can influence the effect of a single technique. Both of these designs begin with tying wet fabric into a bundle and letting it dry in that state to set the wrinkles and creases.

To make the vest opposite, start by cutting a wavy line parallel to the lower edge of the vest pattern for piecing. Create the lower border by alternating two shades of fabric—here, purple cotton. Then decorate the border fabrics with double needle pintucks, using a different thread color in each needle. Fuse the crumpled fabric to a lightweight backing to hold the pleats and creases in place, and embellish it with lines of machine embroidery stitching, using thread colors taken from the print. For a finishing touch, couch twisted strands of yarn, also in colors of the print, onto the piecing seam.

For the vest at left, pleats are stitched and embellished with the machine's straight stitch in varied thread colors. On the right front is a curvy inlaid stripe of pintucked cotton. The inlay is embellished with double needle pintucks stitched with contrasting thread, and it's bordered by couched yarn in colors of the print. The back of this vest is an enlargement of the design used for the front inlay—solid purple fabric with wavy rows of double needle pintucks worked in all of the colors of the print fabric on the front. Buttons are covered in the same purple pintucked fabric.

DESIGN
Becky Brodersen

SEWING AIDS, SEE:

*Fabric manipulation,
page 149
Piecing and patchwork,
page 150
Couching, page 142*

Becky   Brodersen

DESIGN
Lori Kerr

With its muted color, this vest provided a perfect playground for design experimentation. Appliqué motifs, some cut from shiny fabrics for contrast, and some pieced together for variety, exhibit all sorts of shapes and textures. Each is positioned on the vest, then stitched in a free-spirited manner with decorative thread. Triangular shapes around the neckline are sewn into the lining seam, then given a garnish of decorative stitching.

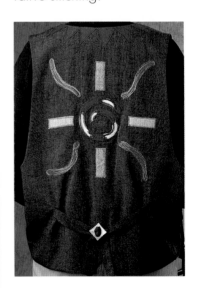

SEWING AIDS, SEE:

Appliqué, page 136
Machine embroidery,
page 147

A small piece of elegant wool tweed, long a member of the designer's household, had never seemed quite suitable for any project. Then one day she looked at the checked pattern on the diagonal—the next day she had a magnificent new vest!

The fabric is so firmly woven that even when cut on the bias it doesn't stretch or sag, but it still conforms to the body in an attractive way. The vest is unlined; lining or underlining would interfere with the fabric's bias shaping.

As shown in figure 1, the front pieces are extended slightly to follow the check pattern of the fabric, and a long vertical dart is added for shaping. (See page 24 for more information on making pattern alterations.) The back is cut on the straight grain. Wool braid finishes the edges all around, while twisted wool cord ties the front closed.

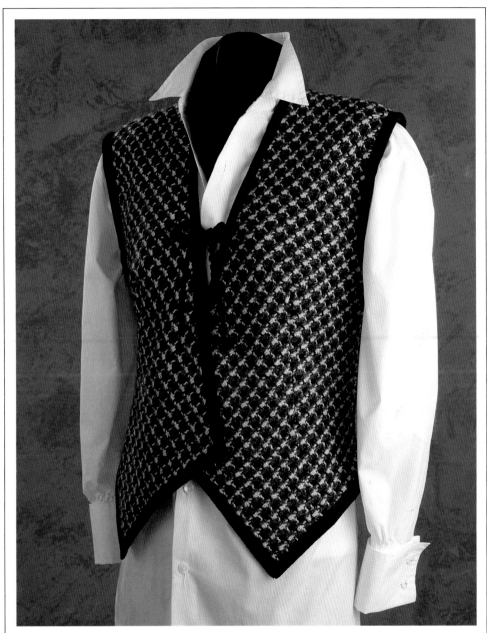

D E S I G N
M a g g i e   R o t m a n

103

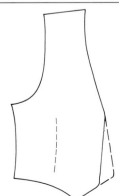

*Figure 1. Extending the front pieces and
adding front darts*

DESIGN
Robbie Spivey

he designer's experimentation with silk dyeing resulted in fabrics and colors as soft as a spring day. In her vest, she uses a patchwork of blues and greens for the sky and grassland, and embroiders the edges with blanket stitch. Small flowers, embroidered with silk threads, dot the landscape. A lily-of-the-valley provides a focal point; it's appliquéd in place and embellished with hand-worked embroidery.

SEWING AIDS, SEE:

Piecing and patchwork,
page 150
Appliqué, page 136
Embroidery, page 146

A distinctive cotton print, with a Japanese theme, found ideal companions in two cotton plaids of the same color family. The vest is reversible. On the print side are small pockets with red plaid trim and off-center tabs. On the other side, appliquéd butterflies are stitched to the red plaid background. Black plaid edge binding is visible from both sides.

Fabric scraps make up the butterfly motif, which is repeated on the sides and back. Lavish embellishment with machine embroidery gives each butterfly texture and sheen. A double row of antique buttons—no two alike—adorns the front.

105

DESIGN
L o r i   K e r r

SEWING AIDS, SEE:

Appliqué, page 136   *Machine embroidery, page 147*   *Pockets, page 153*

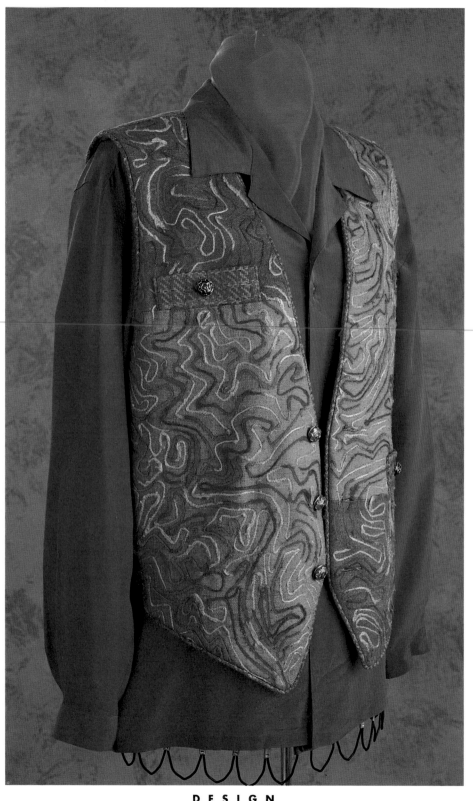

The discovery of a skein of variegated yarn, colored to match a treasured piece of matka silk tweed, led to the creation of this dramatic vest. The tweed fabric was used for the vest's back and for accents on the front: small pockets sewn into the piecing seams and corded piping around the vest's edges. The front began as two solid colors, but when the couched yarn was applied, it became a vibrant pattern of swirls.

D E S I G N
Mary Parker

SEWING AIDS, SEE:

Piecing and patchwork,
page 150
Couching, page 142
Pockets, page 153

The pattern of this handwoven silk was designed to accommodate the lines of the vest. Such a distinctive fabric doesn't need embellishment; it creates a superb garment just as it is! Fused glass buttons, the only ornamentation, echo the lines of the fabric pattern. If you don't happen to be a weaver yourself, you can often purchase someone else's handiwork in the form of shawls, table runners and cloths, or throws. For more information on sewing handwoven fabrics, see page 150.

DESIGN
Suzanne Gernandt

The designer's own fabric is a networked silk and cotton twill, woven of hand-dyed yarns. Its subtle beauty calls for the simplest of designs.

The asymmetrical half-collar is cleverly designed: It's simply an extension of the front neckline that's turned back and sewn into the shoulder seam. (See figure 2 on page 26.) A facing cut to follow the front outer edge/collar lines creates the visible portion of the collar.

At the front closure are four handmade ceramic beads. Braided cord made from the weaving yarn forms the button loops. The back is silk, dyed to match the woven fabric, and features three small pleats at the waist-line to hold in fullness.

DESIGN
Betty Carlson

SEWING AIDS, SEE:

Pattern alterations, page 24
Sewing handwoven fabrics,
page 150

A pretty cotton batik with colorful stripes just begs for some special treatment. Here it's pleated to hide the brighter colored stripes, then pleated in the opposite direction to reveal them in a diagonal pattern across the front. First the lengthwise tucks are stitched on the right side of the fabric. Then, where the pleats are folded back, a line of horizontal stitching holds them in place. See page 149 for more ideas on fabric manipulation.

DESIGN
Becky Brodersen

Sometimes it's a fabric's potential as much as its prettiness that compels you to take it home. This cotton ikat is perfect for experimenting with fabric tucking and pleating.

Here, tucks in two different sizes are made with a fabric pleater. These are secured in place with a variety of machine embroidery stitches, worked in rayon and metallic threads, that add accents of color at the same time.

The left side of the vest features a patchwork of pleating techniques. The samplers are pieced together, stitched to a lightweight cotton backing, then bordered with satin stitch over the seams.

The vest's back and lining are the same ikat fabric—used just as it comes off the bolt. Purchased silver piping trims the outer edges and armholes.

SEWING AIDS, SEE:

*Fabric manipulation,
page 149
Piecing and patchwork,
page 150*

DESIGN
M a r y P a r k e r

The cotton print is enchanting, but could be overwhelming in too large a quantity. The modest size of a vest is just right. The fabric needs little in the way of embellishment, so just a plain corded piping is added to finish the edges.

The back takes two colors from the print to simulate the Caribbean sea and sky. For the belt, motifs are cut from the print and bonded to a firm fabric to stiffen them. The edges are oversewn with satin stitch, and the ends of the belt sewn to the vest. Small embroidered bubbles ascend to the surface.

SEWING AIDS, SEE:

Appliqué, page 136
Piping, page 145

DESIGN
the author

INCORPORATING SEVERAL FABRICS INTO A SINGLE GARMENT IS A PERFECT VEST-MAKING TECHNIQUE. PATCHWORK THAT WOULD BE OVERWHELMING IN A JACKET OR SKIRT PRODUCES A VEST THAT'S NOTHING SHORT OF SENSATIONAL.

NEARLY EVERY SEWER CHERISHES A SMALL HOARD OF LEFTOVERS FROM OTHER PROJECTS, AND MANY OF US HAVE A SMALL STACK OF REMNANT BARGAINS IN PIECES ALWAYS A LITTLE TOO SMALL FOR ANYTHING. FOR THOSE OF US WHO CAN'T THROW AWAY EVEN THE SMALLEST SCRAPS, PIECED VESTS NOT ONLY PROVIDE THE OPPORTUNITY TO MIX MATERIALS IN AN INNOVATIVE WAY, BUT THEY ALSO ALLOW US THE VIRTUOUS FEELING OF HAVING ACTUALLY USED SOME OF OUR ACCUMULATED WEALTH.

THE DESIGNS IN THIS CHAPTER REPRESENT VERY DIFFERENT METHODS FOR FABRIC PIECING. THEY ALL HAVE ONE TRAIT IN COMMON: ALTHOUGH EACH FINISHED VEST APPEARS TO BE A HAPPY ACCIDENT OF FABRIC COMBINATION, EVERY ONE IS IN FACT THE RESULT OF MUCH PLANNING AND EXPERIMENTATION.

This vest began with a lament that's been repeated at one time or another by every sewer in the world: "I didn't have quite enough fabric to...." The designer searched out a compatible print with a similar African theme, interchanged motifs between the two, and ended up with a vest far more interesting than the single fabric might have produced. Fabric shortage is the mother of creativity!

To add color to the black and white print, some of the motifs are embroidered with colors from the green/brown print. Other motifs are cut from the black and white fabric, embellished with color, and appliquéd to the green/brown side. The vest is reversible, with the unadorned green/brown print as the inside fabric. Armholes and outer edges are topstitched with pearl rayon thread—in the bobbin—using a zigzag stitch. In place of buttons, ornamental dangles made up of assorted beads are sewn along the front opening.

SEWING AIDS, SEE:

Appliqué, page 136
Machine embroidery, page 147

112

113

DESIGN
Lori Kerr

Just the vest for festive evenings, the effect is one of subtle glitter. Richly colored stripes of taffeta and brocade are pieced on a serger, using brightly colored metallic threads. The back of the vest is a dignified solid black.

To piece the strips, use the serger's two-thread option. Thread the looper with decorative metallic thread, and use standard sewing thread in the needle. For a serger without the two-thread capability, matching sewing thread or invisible nylon thread can be used in the other looper. When joining the strips, take care to position the pieces so that the decorative thread will always appear on the right side of the fabric.

Cut enough strips for the width of the vest pieces, plus a little extra at each side for seam allowances and to allow some leeway in the arrangement when laying out the pattern. Allow about 2" (5 cm) extra in length.

After all the strips are pieced, press the seams flat, and topstitch on the sewing machine with invisible or matching thread to secure the seams. The piecing seams could also be flat-locked, but the seams would not be as strong.

For vest makers without sergers, this look can be duplicated by piecing strips on the sewing machine. Topstitch over the seams with a decorative stitch, sewing from the wrong side with metallic thread in the bobbin.

SEWING AIDS, SEE:

Piecing and patchwork,
page 150
Machine embroidery,
page 147

115

DESIGN
Mary Parker

DESIGN
the author

ton. At the lower left, a pocket is incorporated into the seam, with a tab sewn into the pocket/lining seam. One patch over the right side seam serves as a belt carrier.

The belt is made of two long tubes turned right side out. Each is folded diagonally at both ends so that when the two tubes are placed side by side, they form a point at each end. The tubes are stitched together lengthwise, leaving a small section open where needed for a buttonhole. The belt extends around the back to just past the center, and it buttons in the fullness at both sides of the center back.

The back is constructed of two pieces, with an off-center vertical seam. A row of hand-embroidered feather stitch parallels the seam. The vest is edged with corded linen piping, and it's lined in a cotton print fabric.

A scrap-saver's delight, this pieced linen vest was designed to use up some of the leftover fabric amassed over the years.

Two pieces on the right shoulder are joined by fagoting (see figure 20 on page 147), then treated as a single piece. For the piece at the center right, an extra seam allowance was added and folded under. Three buttonholes—all strictly ornamental—are worked along the folded lower edge, and each is fastened with a horn but-

SEWING AIDS, SEE:

*Piecing and patchwork,
page 150
Embroidery, page 146
Buttons and buttonholes,
page 139
Pockets, page 153*

Some simple pattern changes have given this vest its interesting lines: One side of the upper front is extended, and the other has a matching piece cut out. Combined with the arrangement of fabric pieces, this creates an intriguing crossover "collar." The lower front edges extend outward and are rounded at the bottom. A wonderful mix of fabrics is used: silks, wool crepe, polyester, acetate, and cotton sateen. On both front and back, the upper part of the vest (the "collar") is pieced in Seminole patchwork style, and the lower part in crazy quilt, with decorative cord dividing the two. The patchwork is lavishly embellished with metallic and lustrous rayon threads in different colors and stitch patterns.

SEWING AIDS, SEE:

Piecing and patchwork,
page 150
Machine embroidery,
page 147

DESIGN
Lori Kerr

117

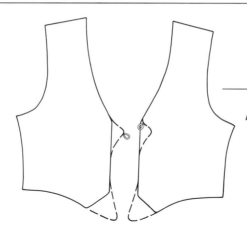

Figure 1. Simple pattern alterations to create interesting lines

DESIGN
P a t   T a y l o r

This designer has turned from quilting to vest making, and she dyes most of her own fabrics to get the soft hues and subtle color variations that work so well in patchwork. For each of these two designs she has chosen a single commercially printed fabric for accent and for the lining. Her fabric of choice for the main part of the vest is cotton muslin, a wonderfully workable fabric that is also very inexpensive. She uses fiber-reactive dyes made especially for use with cellulose fibers.

To make the purple vest, the strips are cut on the straight grain of the fabric, then pieced on the diagonal. On the right front, strips of color are overlapped as they are sewn, creating the V shape. Below the striped V, the solid-colored section is also pieced, eliminating the need for sewing a tricky pointed seam. On the right front, two "prairie points" are tucked into one of the piecing seams for interest.

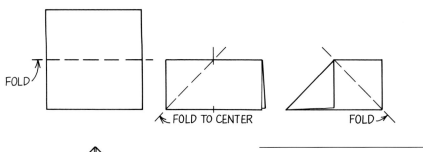

FOLD

FOLD TO CENTER

FOLD

SEW

Figure 1.
Making a prairie point

To make a prairie point, cut a square of fabric. Fold it in half on the grainline. Then fold each corner of the folded edge down to meet the raw edge. This produces a triangle with all of the raw edges at its base. (See figure 1.)

On the black vest, notice how the designer has located the detailed area of design toward the center front, keeping the sides in the solid color for a slimming effect when the vest is worn. For more information on piecing and patchwork, see page 150.

DESIGN
Pat Taylor

119

D E S I G N
R o b b i e   S p i v e y

T wo vests are made by the same designer and employ the same techniques, yet each is distinctive because of the materials used. Both vests feature a great variety of fabrics combined with beautiful hand-worked embroidery.

The peach and taupe vest is a textural feast, with silk crepe, wool flannel, satin, brocade, and plain cotton. Carefully placed tiny pearl beads, small beaded medallions, and ribbon rosettes add still more texture. The black vest blends shades and textures for an entirely different effect.

Whether fabrics for patchwork are gleaned from the trunk in grandmother's attic or bought today, the technique has a historic look about it. And since it's practically impossible to duplicate a patchwork piece, every garment is unique to its designer.

SEWING AIDS, SEE:

Appliqué, page 136
Beads and sequins, page 139
Piecing and patchwork,
page 150
Embroidery, page 146

DESIGN
Robbie Spivey

Embroidered cotton ribbon alternates with bright red grosgrain for a design that's very effective, yet quite simple to execute. Ribbons are available in a wonderful array of embroidered, printed, and woven patterns, as well as in many solid colors and textures. There are all sorts of possibilities with this technique.

To accommodate the ribbons' straight lines, several pattern changes must be made. Start by cutting a separate underarm piece wide enough to eliminate the side seam curves and to allow the armhole to be cut straight. Eliminate the overlap at the center front to avoid ribbon placement problems and to allow decorative pewter clasps to be used, in keeping with the Scandinavian design. Additionally, cut the front slightly higher, and cut it straight to the neckline.

The method for constructing this vest is a bit different from that described in the general instructions. The ribbon is sewn right side facing out onto a backing, or foundation fabric, and it's not sewn into any lengthwise seams, which would interfere with the design.

For the backing, use a firmly woven lightweight fabric in a color that matches the darkest ribbon color (it might show through here and there). First cut just the side/underarm pieces from the backing fabric, allowing about 2" (5 cm) extra in length at the lower edge. Fold the seam allowance at the upper edge to the inside; press. Starting at the top of the backing piece, position ribbon strips horizontally, aligning the edge of the first ribbon with the fold of the backing. The ends of the ribbon should extend slightly beyond the edges of the backing (they will be trimmed later). Place each subsequent ribbon right up against the preceding strip so that the edges meet. Let the width of the ribbons determine the finished length of the vest; the ribbon should not be cut lengthwise.

Sew the ribbons to the backing and to each other at the same time using a bridging stitch, if your machine has one, or a fairly narrow zigzag. At the bottom of the piece, leave enough of the backing fabric for a seam allowance, and trim off the excess.

Cut backing for the fronts and back, matching the length to that of the side pieces plus the seam allowances at the lower edges. Fold under and press the seam allowances along the front edges and at the armholes.

Cut the lining to the same pattern, matching the length of the backing.

Working from the center front *seamline,* position the ribbons vertically, laying each strip of ribbon exactly next to the preceding piece. If necessary, cheat a little at the center front and at the side seams so that the ribbon will come out evenly across the piece, ending at the armhole *seamline,* without cutting the ribbon lengthwise. Stitch the ribbons in place as you did for the side pieces. Work the back the same way, starting at the center. Then trim the ribbon ends even with the backing.

Sew the fronts to the side pieces, keeping the edges of the ribbons on the fronts free of the stitching. Sew the back to the sides in the same way. Finally, sew the shoulder seams.

Stitch the ends of the ribbons to the neckline along the seamline. Stitch again inside the seam allowance, 1/8" (3 mm) from the first stitching line. Trim away half the remaining seam allowance, and on the curves, clip the seam allowance to the outer stitching line. Turn under the seam allowance on the inner stitching line; press. Press under the backing seam allowances on both front and back armholes.

Sew the lining fronts and back to the sides. Then sew the shoulder seams. Press under the seam allowances along the front edges and neckline, stitching and clipping the neckline as you did for the vest. Press under the armhole seam allowances.

With right sides together, stitch the lining to the vest along the lower edge, making sure the seamline is even with the bottom of the side pieces. Keep the ribbon on the side pieces free of the seam. Trim and grade the seam allowances; then turn the garment right side out and press.

By hand, stitch the lining to the vest along the front, around the neck-line, and around the armholes, matching the folded edges. Top-stitching will prevent the lining from rolling to the outside. As an alterna-tive, the lining can be basted to the vest, keep-ing the edges exactly even, then edgestitched by machine.

123

DESIGN
Robbie Spivey

Assorted small pieces of very soft silk are hand dyed, cut into strips, and woven into fabric for a very sophisticated vest. The almost jacketlike appearance of the vest results from lengthening the pattern and squaring off the bottom front. (See page 24 for more on making pattern alterations.)

The secret to producing good results with hand-dyeing projects is to use the commercial-quality dyes that are available at craft supply stores. This vest has a spring-time palette: shades of yellow, orange, purple, rose, and green. Additional intermediate hues are created by immersing some pieces into several dye baths.

Once all of the pieces have been dyed, cut them into 4" (10 cm) strips. Then fold the edges of each strip inward to meet at the center, forming a 2" (5 cm) strip with a folded edge at each side.

To maintain its shape, the woven fabric requires a backing. Trace the pattern pieces onto the glue side of *very* lightweight fusible interfacing, and place one of the interfacing pieces on an ironing board, glue side up. Working in one direction, cut lengths of the strips so that they extend slightly beyond the edges of the interfacing piece. Lay them side by side, with the edges just meeting, and pin one end of each strip onto the backing.

Now cut strips of fabric to weave through the pinned pieces. Weave in the new strips at right angles to the first set, making sure that each new strip is right up against its neighbor before pinning it in place.

When the weaving is complete, cover it with a pressing cloth, and steam press it lightly so that the interfacing will adhere to the fabric. Remove the pins; then fuse the fabric to the interfacing thoroughly, according to the interfacing manufacturer's instructions. Stay stitch around all of the edges.

After cutting the fabric according to the pattern pieces, construct the vest according to the basic instructions. This one is lined with green silk.

For the front band, make a single vertical strip that is interwoven with short horizontal strips. Fold under the horizontal pieces on both ends, and stitch them invisibly to the vest.

125

DESIGN
Maggie Rotman

Making a garment from one's own fabric is a gratifying and heady experience! These designers employ a number of different techniques to produce their materials; some are quite complicated, and others are not. All of their vests exhibit qualities that can translate to other techniques and fabrics, and all have great inspirational value.

The fabrics used for these vest fronts come from the loom of a professional weaver and were created in the manner of a rag rug. She used a plain weave structure with cotton rug for the warp and 1" (2.5 cm) strips of cotton fabric for the weft. A fairly light beat prevents the fabric from becoming too dense and stiff for a comfortable garment. The back of the blue and white vest is the same blue chambray used in the weft, and the lining is a delicate blue and white striped cotton. The multicolored vest has a back and lining of soft ivory-colored cotton and is accented with buttons made of beads.

For nonweavers, the designer suggests searching out old, old cotton rag rugs at flea markets. Once they become too soft and worn for their original purpose, they're just about right for conversion into interesting garments!

With either handwoven or resuscitated rag fabric, the edges of the pieces should be overcast on a serger or sewing machine immediately after cutting. A tape stay at the front and armhole edges prevents these areas from stretching out of shape. Because the fabric is too thick for attractive machine-made buttonholes, decorative corded loops are the best bet. (See page 139 for help with buttons and buttonholes.)

126

DESIGN
Liz Spears

D E S I G N
Liz Spears

DESIGN
Dale Liles

it doesn't ravel. The fabric is very thick, so construction techniques are somewhat different.

The felt used for the gray vest is made from the fleece of Correidale sheep, which is particularly good for garments. It, like all of the felt made by this designer, has been hand dyed with natural dyes. At the time of felting, accents of red and white fleece were incorporated into the gray.

Both the vest and lining are cut without seam allowances. To allow for the felt's greater thickness, silk for the lining is cut slightly wider than the felt, and slightly longer at the front points. Small ease pleats are stitched at the back neckline and front shoulders.

Because felt produces very bulky seams, each vest piece is sewn to its lining before the vest is assembled. On the sides and shoulders, the lined pieces are stitched close to the edge with a machine blind hem stitch that is set at a fairly long stitch length. The side seams and shoulders are sewn with handspun yarn, dyed to match the

Felt making is a very old process and one that most of us have accomplished accidentally by throwing a wool sweater into the hot water wash. The designer calls felt making a "no strings attached" process—it involves no spinning, weaving, or knitting, but converts wool fleece directly to usable material.

Felt is made by arranging layers of carded wool fiber in opposing directions, then basting the layers together. A layer of cheesecloth can be incorporated in the middle to give the wool stability. The wool is immersed in hot water and massaged to encourage the fibers to interlock. Then it's towel

dried, shaped, and left to dry completely. This is merely a simplified version of the process; there are a number of good books available that give all the details.

Wool felt is light in weight, warm, and windproof. A sewer also needs to know that it has little drape or ease, and wool, by interlacing the yarn through the zigzag steps of the blind hem stitches.

Strips of suedelike polyester fabric bind the edges and anchor the button loops. Buttons are reinforced with a small piece of felt under the button on the right side or with a backing button on the inside of the vest.

The brown vest is unlined and reversible. It's pattern incorporates felt that has been dyed in contrasting colors, rolled jelly-roll fashion, then sliced and worked into the fleece. The seams are joined in the same manner described for the gray vest, and the edges are finished with the same technique used for seams.

Handmade felt may be inaccessible to most of us, but these sewing techniques work equally well on other stiff fabrics such as heavy wool melton and boiled wool. And besides, there's always another sweater to wash....

DESIGN
Dale Liles

Individually dyed pieces of cotton muslin create a brilliantly colored fabric when pieced together. (See page 150 for more ideas on piecing and patchwork.) Here the colored squares are assembled with narrow strips to delineate them. The vest's lining is a purchased cotton in deep purple with a mottled pattern.

When custom tinting your own fabrics, always use good quality commercial dyes, which are available from crafts suppliers. Carefully follow the manufacturer's directions to get the best results.

DESIGN
Pat Taylor

arbling is a technique that involves floating thick paints on the surface of water, swirling the colors to create patterns, then laying the fabric carefully on the surface to pick up the design paints. It's fun to try! There isn't enough space here to tell all there is to know about marbling, but there are a number of good books describing the process.

For this vest, six different marbled patterns are interspersed with solid colors in a vibrantly colored patchwork design. (For more information on piecing and patchwork, refer to page 150.) To make the shorter bolero style, the vest pattern is shortened and the front points rounded off (see figure 1 on page 26).

DESIGN
Laura Sims (marbling)
& Becky Orr (patchwork)

DESIGN
Susan   Kinney

While "fabric" may not be an altogether accurate term for the material used for these designs, handmade paper does produce an out-of-the-ordinary vest! The gray vest is made from newspapers and— believe it if you will— dryer lint. The pink striped model is layered paper in several shades, all made by mixing strongly dyed pulp with varying amounts of white pulp and dryer lint.

These may not be your idea of comfort clothing, but paper vests *are* wearable, and they make great conversation starters at parties. Lightweight fabric liners give the vests more stability and make them easier to put on and off. The lining fabric is cut from the pattern, then glued to the paper or fused to it with bonding web.

Simple paper-making projects can be accomplished with materials that are readily available, and there are several good instruction books to get you started.

A serger makes quick work of creating the "ribbons" woven into the fabric for this vest. Strips of ikat-weave silk fabric are edged with decorative threads, with a different color used for each side of the strip. For vest fronts in a medium size, approximately 1-1/4 yards (1.1 m) of fabric are needed for the strips.

Set up the serger for three-thread overlock, using the right needle. Thread the lower looper with regular sewing thread, the upper looper with heavy decorative rayon thread, and the needle with decorative metallic thread.

Cut the fabric into lengthwise strips 1-1/4" (about 3 cm) wide, or serge and cut at the same time. Finish one edge of each strip; then change thread colors in the upper looper and work the other edges.

Weave the strips and fuse them to pieces of very lightweight interfacing that have been cut into the pattern shapes. Stay stitch around the edges before constructing the vest.

DESIGN
Beth Hill

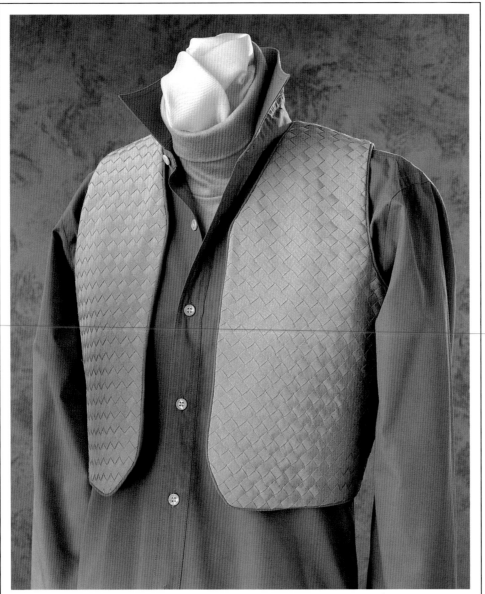

DESIGN
E l m a   J o h n s o n

Narrow grosgrain ribbon, interwoven and positioned diagonally, produces an interesting fabric with wonderful texture. It's a simple technique that has all sorts of possible variations.

Trace the pattern pieces onto the glue side of *very* lightweight fusible interfacing. Place one of the interfacing pieces on an ironing board, glue side up. Working in one direction, cut lengths of ribbon to extend slightly beyond the edges of the interfacing piece, laying them side by side so that the edges just meet. Pin one end of each ribbon firmly in place.

Now cut lengths of ribbon to weave through the pinned ribbons. As you weave, make sure that each ribbon is right up against its neighbor; then pin it in place.

When the weaving is complete, cover the ribbon with a pressing cloth, and steam press the fabric lightly so that the interfacing will adhere. Carefully remove the pins, and fuse the ribbons to the interfacing well, following the interfacing manufacturer's instructions. Stay stitch around all of the edges, and trim your new fabric by the pattern.

The finished vest is a bolero style (see figure 1 on page 26) with corded piping to match its coral-colored lining.

SEWING AIDS, SEE:

Pattern alterations, page 24
Piping, page 145

Perhaps not for everyday wear, and definitely not corporate, these vests are for special occasions that demand an out-of-the-ordinary costume. They may have been inspired by the ancient Greek soldier's cuirass (a vestlike form of body armor), which only proves that history does repeat itself.

While it may be far-fetched to refer to the materials in these two vests as "fabric," they are fine examples of imaginative vest making just the same. The lady's model has a base of hardware cloth onto which assorted found objects have been artfully applied. The front closures, appropriately enough, are screen door hooks. The gentleman's vest is an environmentally correct collection of pop tops, riveted to a copper sheeting background. No further embellishments are required.

DESIGN
Nancy Fleming (h e r s)
and Charlie Covington (h i s)

ADDING YOUR OWN
SPECIAL TOUCHES

APPLIQUÉ

WHEN YOU CUT A DESIGN or shape from one fabric and stitch it onto another, you're doing appliqué. It's that simple! For inspiration, look at the photos on pages 49, 50, 57, 62, 64, 90, 95, and 97. Many of the vests shown in the project section feature appliquéd design. Some are as simple as a motif cut from a print fabric and applied to a solid-colored background. Some are quite ornate and colorful, with elaborate designs made up of several fabrics and richly embellished with embroidery stitches.

When planning an appliqué design, consider the size of the motifs, and keep them in proportion to the garment. Eliminate small details, and work with simple shapes. Rounded corners are easiest to cut and sew. Use appliqué for larger design features, and add machine stitching for the fine lines and embellishments, as in the vest on page 57.

Because of the heavy stitching involved in appliqué, the vest fabric should be underlined with a lightweight fusible or sew-in interfacing to serve as a backing for the stitching. The need for any additional backing depends upon the amount of stitching that will be done. For a few hand-appliquéd motifs on a medium-weight fabric, additional backing is unnecessary if an embroidery hoop is used. For elaborate machine-stitched decorations worked on a larger appliquéd area, a firm backing in addition to the lightweight interfacing is a good idea. In this case, a light fusible interfacing material

A beautiful example of appliqué

might be applied to the entire ground fabric, and a tear-away backing used under the areas to be appliquéd. A spray-on fabric stiffener can be used instead of an underlining. It should first be tested on a fabric sample.

Appliqué can be worked using hand or machine embroidery stitches. (Embroidery techniques are covered in the section beginning on page 146.) No matter which approach you choose, note that the extra stitchery will draw up your fabric to some extent. Cut your fabric slightly larger all around than the pattern piece; then trim it to the pattern after you have completed your appliquéd designs.

Motifs for hand appliqué usually are not backed; they're generally embroidered onto the ground fabric using a hoop. Traditionally, motifs are cut with a narrow seam allowance around all the edges. The seam allowance is turned under and the motif stitched invisibly to its ground. If a decorative stitch, such as blanket or satin stitch, is used to apply the motifs, the edges need not be turned under but can be dabbed with liquid fray retardant to prevent raveling.

For machine application, motifs cut from lightweight fabrics should be backed. Paper-backed fusible web is a good material for this purpose. Begin by fusing the web to the motif fabric. Then trace or draw the motifs wrong side up on the backing. Cut the designs from the bonded fabric, peel off the backing and press the patterns onto the vest fabric. Motifs applied with this material need stitching only for decoration. Note that this method can stiffen the garment considerably if large areas are appliquéd.

An embroidery hoop is a boon for machine appliqué when stiff backings aren't used. Just place your fabric in the hoop, and position it for stitching on the machine. The hoop helps prevent the stitches from puckering the ground fabric, especially when design fabrics are applied with dense embroidery such as a satin stitch.

An appliqué foot is available for many machines. Some are clear plastic, and all have a groove on the underside that allows the foot to slide freely over heavy stitching. This foot also exerts slightly less pressure on the fabric, making turns easier.

No matter what method you use for appliqué, it is always a good idea to experiment on scraps with the fabrics, threads, and stitches you plan to use in the final design.

BACK BELTS

BECAUSE THE VEST PATTERN is cut straight across the back, you may like to add a belt or elastic at the waistline to gather in some of the fullness. A belt can be as much a design feature as it is practical. With a wonderful antique pearl buckle, a simple belt becomes elegant. Belts also can be made of complementary fabric or in complementary colors or patterns.

The finished length of the elastic or belt should be about 1" to 2" (2.5 to 5 cm) less than the fabric width it will cover, depending upon the individual design and body shape. Another way to measure is to make the finished length of the belt (set-in or elastic) slightly less than one-third the width of the total vest back width measurement. A back belt should be positioned at, or slightly above, the waistline.

■ Elastic in self casing ■

AFTER THE LINING has been sewn to the vest, but before the side seams are closed, a strip of 1" (2.5 cm) elastic can be stitched into the back. Mark the placement of the casing, allowing the opening to be 1/2" (1.3

Elastic belt in self casing

cm) wider than the elastic. Then stitch parallel lines across the vest, through both the vest and the lining. After cutting the elastic to desired the length—1" or 2" (2.5 or 5 cm) shorter than casing plus 1" (2.5 cm) for seam allowances—insert the elastic into the casing. Stitch securely across one end, through all the layers; stretch and stitch across the other end.

■ Add-on elastic casing ■

A CASING CAN BE ADDED after the vest is complete, either as a decorative feature or because you didn't think to do it sooner. Depending upon the effect you want to create, it can be stitched to the inside or the outside of the vest. Measure for the casing and elastic as in the method above.

Cut a piece of fabric 1" (2.5 cm) wider and 2" (5 cm) longer than you want the finished casing to be. Fold under the ends 1/2" (1.3 cm); stitch. Fold under another 1/2" and press. Then press under 1/2" along each long edge. Position the casing on the vest, and stitch the long edges close to the folds.

Insert the elastic so that it's even with one end of the casing. Stitch securely about 1/2" (1.3 cm) in from the end. Then trim the elastic short of the end of the casing, and stitch the end of the casing close to the fold. Finally, stretch the elastic to the other end of the casing and stitch the same way.

■ Side seam belt ■

THIS IS THE SIMPLEST BELT to make, and it can be varied

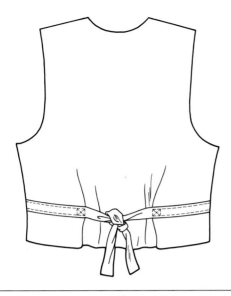

Figure 1. Side seam belt

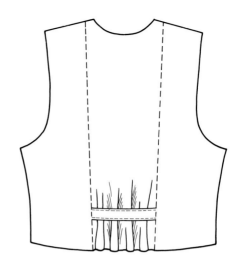

Figure 2. Pieced back with belt

in any number of ways. As shown in figure 1, it can be stitched in place part way across the back and tied at the center. A buckle can be added or fastened with D-rings. A different effect results when the belt is cut as one piece, shorter than the back, with button-holes sewn in, then buttoned to the vest. Alternatively, it can be made using a contrasting color, braided cord, yarn, or a different fabric.

If you have a good tube turner, the belt sections can be sewn as tubes, closed at one end, then turned right side out. Without this tool it's easier to fold under the raw edges at one end and the long sides of each piece, then topstitch them closed.

For a tie belt, cut each piece twice the desired width plus two seam allowances. In length each should be about three-quarters the width of the vest back. The belt sections can be shorter if you use a buckle or D-rings.

Baste the belt sections to the back side seamlines before sewing the sides closed. Topstitch each belt section to the vest about a third of the way across the vest from each side, if you like. Alternatively, stitch across each section vertically at the one-third point.

Pin the ends out of the way so that they won't be caught inadvertently in the stitching when you sew the sides.

■ Pieced back with belt ■

THE VEST BACK can be cut vertically into approximate thirds, adding design interest as well as providing seams into which a belt can be placed. (See figure 2.) Remember to add seam allowances on all of the pieces where cuts are made. For a one-piece belt, calculate the finished belt length 1" or 2" (2.5 or 5 cm) shorter than the width of vest it will span. For a two-piece belt that will tie or buckle, add the desired length to each section.

If back darts are added (see page 26), this style belt can be stitched into the darts. Slash the dart fold line at the waist, and incorporate the belt end into the dart stitching line.

■ Add-on belt ■

BELTS MADE LIKE THOSE described above can be finished on both ends, then sewed or attached with buttons to the right side of the lined vest. An alternative is to cut a motif from printed fabric, stiffen it, and overcast the edges. Then stitch it to the vest at the ends of the belt to cover a double line of gathering stitches. See the photo on page 111 for an example.

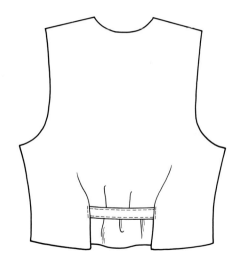

Figure 3. Afterthought belt

■ Afterthought belt ■

THIS ONE, TOO, can be added after the vest has been completed. Make a one- or two-piece belt as described in any of the above methods. Mark the area it will span. On the outside of the vest, pinch a pleat about 1/2" (1.3 cm) deep at each end of the span. Fold them toward the center back and press. Insert the unfinished ends of the belt into the pleats, and stitch securely through all layers. (See figure 3.)

As shown in the photo on page 108, fullness at the back waist can be taken in with pleats or tucks instead of a belt.

BEADS AND SEQUINS

WHETHER YOU HAVE just a sprinkling or an elaborate overall pattern, sequins or beads provide an unusual accent to a vest design.

No special supplies are needed for sewing sequins or most beads as small accents. With very small beads, such as seed beads, the holes may not be large enough to accommodate a standard sewing needle. For these, a thinner beading needle is required to pass through the tiny holes. Sew them with a good quality polyester thread.

If the design calls for large areas of beading, a backing should be used with the fabric to support their weight. A string of beads used for decoration should be secured with couching stitches, as shown in figure 4.

Figure 4. Couching a string of beads

To sew sequins in place, take a stitch up through the sequin, over its edge, and back down through the fabric. The stitches will be visible but can be worked with clear nylon thread. An alternative, if you want no stitches to show, is to use a small glass bead above each sequin. Take a stitch up through the fabric, sequin, and bead, around one edge of the bead, and back down through the sequin and fabric.

BUTTONS AND BUTTONHOLES

PART OF YOUR VEST'S DESIGN includes deciding what kind of closures you will use. Some closure styles, such as the decorative clasps shown in the photos on pages 91 and 123, require you to eliminate the overlap at the center front when cutting out the vest. Loop buttonholes are sewn into the front vest/lining seam or into the front edge binding. Machine-made buttonholes and corded loops can be worked after the vest has been constructed.

You also have the option of leaving off the buttons and buttonholes altogether if you don't want them, or if the thought of making a buttonhole gives you hives. Most vests are never buttoned anyway.

For some reason, there is usually an uneven number of buttons down the front of a garment. Remember, too, that a woman's vest traditionally has the buttons on the left side, a man's on the right. Designer Pat Taylor, a professional vest maker, says "Women will button, zip, hook, and snap from all sides and angles. Men simply stare blankly if the buttons aren't on the right side."

■ Buttons ■

A VEST IS A PERFECT SITE for the display of an outrageous button or two. Many of the vests in this book feature out-of-the-ordinary buttons, and buttons that are not buttons at all. Beads make interesting buttons, either used singly or in combinations, as do small shells. The vest on page 113 has small groups of beads, no two alike, where buttons are usually found.

If you can't locate buttons that are up to the sensational standard of your vest design, consider making them yourself. Polymer clay, a modelling compound, makes wonderful buttons. It's available in many blendable colors and is hardened by baking at a low temperature in a standard oven. Buttons were custom-made of polymer clay to match the fabric design in the vest on page 72. Craft stores carry this and other button-worthy materials, and many sell button shanks that can be glued in place with two-part epoxy.

Even the old standard fabric-covered buttons can be most intriguing with a little embellishment. In the vest shown on page 100, the buttons are covered with fabric that sports a pintuck, repeating the design of the inlay on the vest front. A very small motif can be embroidered by hand or by machine on the fabric before it is cut to button-covering size.

If you use heirloom buttons for your vest, or if the buttons are simply fragile or made of unusual materials, it might be best to attach them to the garment in a temporary fashion. Then they can be removed before laundering or before being exposed to a dry cleaner's button demolition equipment. Small safety pins with a jog in the pin end work well, if you can find them. Another option for shank buttons is the type of pin—shaped like a small bobby pin—sometimes used with uniform coat buttons. With these, a tiny buttonhole is worked on the button side of the vest, and the button shank is slipped through it. A shank button can also be sewn to a small backing button, which is slipped through a small buttonhole on the button side of the garment. This is a good method to use with reversible garments.

Consider the weight of the buttons you choose. If the vest is made of lightweight fabric, heavy buttons will pull the front all askew. If you're really set on such a combination, use a strip of heavy nonwoven interfacing between the vest and lining on the button side. With any fabric, heavy buttons work best if a small backing button is sewn behind each one on the underside of the garment.

■ Machine buttonholes ■

IT IS ESSENTIAL to have some kind of interfacing behind machine-made buttonholes. This both keeps the stitching from puckering and helps the buttonhole foot work smoothly. If the vest will not be interfaced, or if just a very light underlining is used, place a strip of tear-away backing against the inside of the vest under the buttonhole area. After working the buttonholes, tear away the backing from around the stitching.

Stitching a buttonhole over gimp cord strengthens it and makes it look nice besides. See your machine instruction manual for directions. Buttonholes also can be worked with decorative threads to make them a design feature.

Always make a test buttonhole on scrap fabric, using exactly the same layers and fabrics that are in your garment.

■ Loop buttonholes ■

ALL OF THESE EXTEND past the center front edge. They can be made of the main vest fabric or with an accent fabric, and there are several ways to make them. Most are attached when the front vest/lining seam is sewn. They're placed with the ends of the loops aligned with the raw edges of the fabric, and

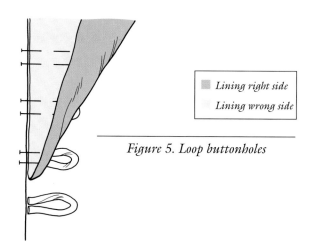

| Lining right side |
| Lining wrong side |

Figure 5. Loop buttonholes

the loops themselves face toward the inside. (Refer to figure 5.) Measure the button to determine the length of loop needed, and add a seam allowance at each end.

Bias loops. Start by cutting a long bias strip of fabric. The width will depend on the thickness of the fabric and how adept you are at tube turning. (A long bodkin with a latch hook at one end is useful for this task. See the photo on page 8 for examples of tube turning tools.) Plan for a finished tube about 1/4" to 3/8" (6 to 10 mm) wide. Fold the bias strip lengthwise, stitch the long edges together, and turn it right side out. Then cut it to the lengths you need, adding a seam allowance at each end. Baste the loops to the vest front, and stitch as described in the section above.

Thick yarn or cord can be inserted into the tube before it's cut into sections. This will help the loop keep its nice three-dimensional shape.

Folded and stitched loops. With heavy fabrics it may be difficult to turn sewn tubes to make fabric loops. Try this instead: Cut a strip of fabric on the lengthwise grain, and fold it in half. Then fold the raw edges to the center and press. Edgestitch both long sides. Cut the finished strip into sections, and sew them in place as described above.

Continuous button loops. Commercially made decorative cord, such as rattail braid, creates attractive button loops. When choosing a cord, look for one

with a thickness appropriate for the size of your buttons. Most of these cords are made of rayon, which is somewhat slippery and has a tendency to pull out of the seams. To prevent this, measure as you would for the other button loops, but don't cut the cord into sections. Instead, pin the cord into the seam as one continuous strip, as shown in figure 6.

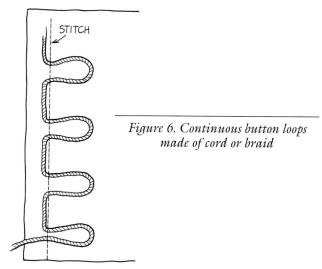

STITCH

Figure 6. Continuous button loops made of cord or braid

141

Fold-over loops. Designer Karen Swing uses this clever button loop on her quilted vests. (See her vest on page 75.) The vest is reversible, and this loop

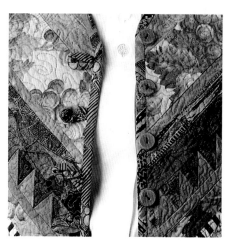

An example of fold-over loops

works from either side of the garment. The loops lie flat and away from the front edge of the garment when not in use, then flip over the edge to button. They are sewn into the front edge binding, with the ends of the loop overlapped.

Cord loops. Designer Liz Spears must be credited for this technique. It's far superior to the common finger-crocheted variety that torques itself into a full nelson around the button to make unbuttoning it an Olympic-scale challenge. Try this, and you'll never turn back. These loops are made after you've finished constructing the vest.

After marking the beginning and end positions of each loop on the edge of the vest, thread an embroidery needle with light cord, such as pearl cotton or crochet thread. Take a few small back stitches on the wrong side of the edge to secure the thread. Then take a stitch through all the fabric layers, and loop across to the end point, leaving a loop large enough to pass over the button with a bit of room to spare. Stitch through the fabric again, and make another loop alongside the first. Take another stitch and make a third loop.

Now work buttonhole stitch (see figure 13, page 146) around the triple-strand loop, *but* make one stitch from the front of the loop, the next from the back, alternating until the cord loop is covered. This button loop *will* lie flat.

COUCHING

COUCHING IS A MEANS of applying yarn or cord to fabric by sewing over it with a stitch that straddles the yarn. Couching can completely change a fabric's appearance, as you can see with the vests on pages 51 and 106.

Couching can be worked with a plain zigzag stitch or with an intricate decorative stitch. Use clear nylon thread to make the stitching invisible, or choose thread in a contrasting color to produce interesting textures and patterns on the fabric. The idea is to stitch over the cord or yarn, but not into it, so that it isn't flattened by the stitching. It may help to loosen the upper thread tension slightly.

All sorts of materials can work with the couching technique. Try yarns, decorative cording, thin braid, or several different heavy threads that have been twisted together.

DYEING AND PAINTING FABRIC

WITH THE EXCELLENT CHOICE of fabric paints and dyes available, there is simply no reason to settle for fabric colors or patterns that aren't quite what you want.

A good craft supplier has dyes and paints to suit many fabrics and techniques. Once the province of experienced fiber artists only, commercial-quality fabric dyes and paints that produce excellent results are now widely available and easy to use.

Embellishing with acrylic paints and fabric paints

Fabric dyes come in a range of colors and are formulated for the specific fiber content of different fabrics. Keep in mind that they are chemicals, and carefully follow the instructions for their use.

Playing with fabric paints can be a rewarding experience and too much fun to be left to children! There are many different kinds available, and like dyes, these paints are designed for specific techniques and fabrics. They are not at all difficult to use. For general use, heat-set paints work with many fabrics, and the colors can be mixed for any hue desired. They can be brushed on, used with stencils, or thickened and applied with stamps. There are special paints, designed to bleed, that are made especially for use on lightweight silks.

Fabric marking pens are another medium for creating custom-patterned fabrics. They are available in many colors, including dazzling fluorescents. Heat-setting is not required, but the colors fade less if the finished work is washed in cold water and line dried.

Fabrics that will be dyed, painted, or colored with markers must first be laundered to remove any surface finishes that could cause uneven penetration of the colors.

Again, take advantage of the local craft store for advice on using these materials. Spend time investigating the vast array of products available to see what will work best for your design.

EDGE FINISHES FOR VESTS

THE DESIGNERS HAVE USED several different methods to finish the outer edges and armholes of the vests shown in this book. The finish you want to use will determine which construction method you use to make your vest. With the standard method, the edges can be topstitched, or piping can be sewn into the vest/lining seam. If the edges will be bound with a braid or bias trim, the vest and lining can be sewn with wrong sides together, using the alternate construction method described on page 31.

For a traditional finish, use decorative trims or piping around the outer edges and neckline, and simply topstitch the armholes. Instructions for making and sewing piping begin on page 145.

■ Topstitching and edgestitching ■

TOPSTITCHING AND EDGESTITCHING are done after the lining has been sewn to the vest and the side seams closed. The stitching is both decorative and functional. It gives the garment a professionally finished look, and it keeps the lining from rolling to the outside. Topstitching is traditionally worked about 1/4" (6 mm) from the garment edge; edgestitching is simply a line of topstitching that is very close to the edge of the garment. Topstitching gives the garment a slightly sportier look. Edgestitching is nice with dressier garments and with designs where topstitching would interfere with the design lines.

For professional-looking topstitching, select a stitch length appropriate to the thickness of the fabric: use a rather short stitch for thin fabrics and a longer one for thicker fabrics. Choose some point on the presser foot or the machine's stitch plate against which to line up the garment edge. Don't sew too slowly, as this can cause uneven stitches. While you're sewing, look at a point in the stitching path slightly ahead of the needle location, just as when you're driving your car you look at a point toward which you're heading, not where the car is at the moment. When stitching around curves, stop every inch or so (every few centimeters) with the needle in the fabric; raise, then lower the presser foot to prevent any distortion of the top layer of fabric.

Heavier thread that's designed for topstitching makes an attractive finish for heavier fabrics. If it's unavailable, two strands of regular sewing thread can be used instead. There are special needles designed for heavier or doubled threads. Called "topstitching needles," they have larger eyes in proportion to the needle size.

Topstitching need not be restricted to straight stitch with matching thread! Using decorative threads—perhaps metallic—and/or a decorative stitch may serve to complement your vest design.

■ Braid trim ■

DECORATIVE FOLDOVER BRAID, available in a number of materials and in many colors, can provide an attractive edge finish. With prefolded trims, one edge is usually folded short of the other. The short edge goes on the right side of the fabric to ensure that when the trim is stitched on the right side, the underside will be caught in the line of stitching. (See figure 7.)

On curved edges, such as the neckline and armholes, ease the vest edge to the braid so that the edges won't ripple when the braid is in place. If it's your first experience with sewing braid, you might "baste" the braid in place by lightly bonding the

A simple but elegant braid trim

braid to the wrong side of the garment with a piece of fusible web every two or so inches (about 5 cm), or by using a spot of fabric glue to hold it in place. Begin and end each strip of braid at some inconspicuous point on the vest. At the end, fold under about 1/2" (1.3 cm), and overlap the starting point.

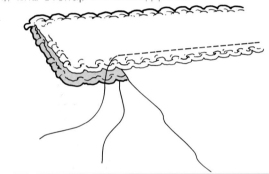

Figure 7. Attaching braid trim

■ Bias binding ■

An EDGING MADE with one of the fabrics used in your vest can give a custom finish to your garment. Since most edges of the vest are curved, edging strips should be cut

*Bias binding
with a complementary fabric*

on the bias so that they will conform to the curves without pleating. Natural fiber fabrics work best; they shape more smoothly than synthetics.

If you plan to use this technique more than once in your lifetime, invest in a bias tape maker (see the photo on page 8). This marvelous gadget folds the bias strip as you press. Bias fabric strips can be cut accurately and easily with a rotary cutter, mat, and clear, gridded ruler.

Measure the edges you wish to bind. Cut bias strips to equal this measurement plus the seam allowances. If you need to piece the strips, add several inches extra. In width, the strips should measure four times the desired finished width of the binding, or the width suggested in the instructions with your tape maker. A finished binding of 1/2" to 5/8" (1.3 to 1.6 cm) is good.

Join the ends of the pieces to make a single strip slightly longer than your edge measurement, as shown in figure 8. Trim the seam

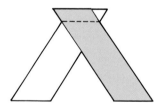

Figure 8. Joining the ends of bias strips

allowances to 1/4" (6 mm) and press them open. With the tape maker, pull the strip through, pressing the folds. Then fold the strip almost along the center, so that one outer edge extends slightly beyond the other, as with the commercial braid trim above.

Without a tape maker, fold the long raw edges together and press, trying not to stretch the strip. Unfold; then fold the raw edges in to the center crease, and press again. Refold and press near the center to offset the outer edges slightly, as with the braid trim, above.

Sew the bias tape to the vest edges following the instructions for decorative braid trim.

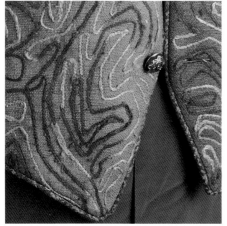

Custom-made piping

WHETHER PUR-CHASED READY TO INSTALL or custom made to match, piping makes an elegant finish for a vest's outer edges, and it can provide an attractive decorative trim for a piecing seam. Piping made to use as an edge trim is usually corded to keep it nicely round. Piping cord is available in several diameters and can be found at most fabric stores. A smallish one is best for use on garments. Purchased piping has an attached welting that is ready to sew into a seam. Fabric-covered piping is available in a few colors; decorative welted cord comes in all sorts of colors and combinations.

As an edging for a vest, piping is usually used just for the outer edges, with the armholes topstitched. It may be applied just to the front edges and neckline, stopping at the side seams, or it may extend all the way around the edge of the vest.

To make corded piping, first measure the edge to be trimmed, and add about 6" (15 cm). In width, strips should be cut the diameter of the cord plus 1-1/4" (3.2 cm). Piece strips of bias fabric to the length of your measurement as described in the instructions for bias edging, above.

Wrap the bias strip right side out around the cord, keeping the fabric edges even. With a piping foot or zipper foot on the machine, stitch the fabric in place, keeping the stitching as close as possible to the cord without stitching through it.

To stitch the piping to the vest, start at the side seamline with the end of the piping in the seam allowance so that the cord crosses the seamline at the lower edge exactly at its intersection with the side seamline, as shown in figure 9. Notch the piping seam allowance near this point so that the piping will curve smoothly. Stitch the piping in place, aligning the piping stitching line with the vest seamline, and stitching over the piping stitching line. Ease the piping around corners, clipping and notching the piping seam allowance in toward the stitching as necessary to allow the piping to lie flat.

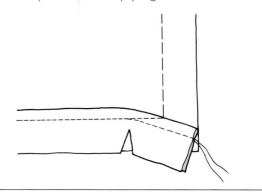

Figure 9. Stitching the end of the piping

145

When you reach the end point, sew the piping into the seamline as you did at the beginning, and cut off any excess. On the ends of the piping, open the piping seam back to the vest stitching line, and clip out the cording to the seamline as shown in figure 10. Trim and clip the seam

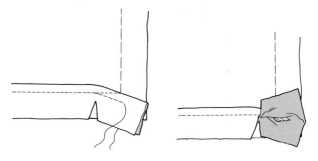

Figure 10. Opening the piping seam and clipping the cord

allowances all around so that the piping will lie flat. On outer curves, such as the front points, cut notches at close intervals almost to the stitching line. On inward curves, as around the armholes, clip almost to the stitching.

Press the stitching line, taking care not to flatten the piping. Then sew the piped vest to the lining, stitching on the piping stitching line.

EMBROIDERY

THERE ARE COUNTLESS WAYS to employ embroidery as a decorative element in a vest design. Because the area of a vest is relatively small, someone fond of hand embroidery could cover an

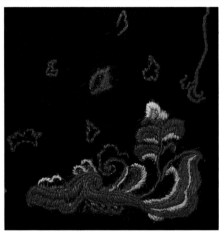

*T*raditional Norwegian hand embroidery

entire vest front with stitched designs and still be able to wear the garment in this lifetime. Embroidery can edge pieced areas, embellish appliqué, or act as topstitching. Even a small embroidered motif or two will add zest to a plain design. Many of the vests shown in the photographs feature embroidery in some form.

■ Hand embroidery ■

A LITTLE EMBELLISHMENT with hand-stitched embroidery can convert the simplest vest to a unique work of art. Embroidery can be used to edge appliquéd motifs, as in the vests on pages 65 and 77. It is also beautiful as an adornment for crazy patchwork; see the vests on pages 120 and 121. Even used in just a small area, as with the vest on page 116, it can change the look of the garment.

For hand embroidery, lightweight fabrics should first be backed with a lightweight interfacing material or underlined with light cotton

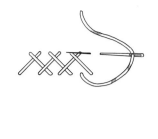

Figure 11. Satin stitch

Figure 12. Herringbone

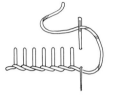

Figure 13. Blanket, or buttonhole stitch

Figure 14. Stem stitch

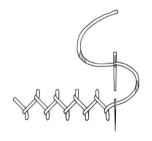

Figure 15. Feather stitch
Bring needle out at X. Insert needle at A, and bring it out at B, holding thread under needle point. Insert needle at C and out at D, holding thread under point.

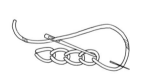

Figure 16. Cretan

Figure 17. Chain stitch

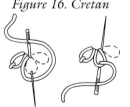

Figure 18. Lazy Daisy

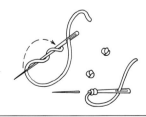

Figure 19. French knot
Bring needle out of fabric, wrap thread twice around needle, and hold firmly. With needle flat against fabric, rotate needle halfway around, and insert it close to starting point.

146

before the stitches are worked. If the garment is pieced, it's easier to do the stitching on individual pieces before assembling them.

A garment piece that will be heavily embroidered should be cut larger—about 2" (5 cm) all around—because the stitching will cause the fabric to draw up. After the embroidery work is finished, recut the piece to the pattern.

Hand embroidery should always be worked in a hoop so that the stitching will not pucker. The only other essential materials are hand embroidery needles and a skein or two of floss.

Volumes have been filled with embroidery designs and stitches. Those that have been used on the vests shown in this book and illustrated here are just a sampling (see figures 11-19).

Fagoting is a technique by which two pieces of fabric are joined together with an embroidery stitch, as in the vest on page 116. The edges of the pieces to be joined should be finished, then folded near the seamline, allowing for the space that will be taken up by the decorative stitching. Then they are basted to graph paper, which keeps them equidistant and provides a guide for evenly spaced stitches.

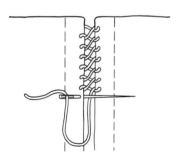

Figure 20. Fagoting

■ Machine embroidery ■

SEWING MACHINE TECHNOLOGY, like that in every other industry, has taken a giant leap in the past few years. The new state-of-the-art machines perform incredible feats and can produce an unlimited vari-

ety of stitch patterns. The increased capability for, and interest in, decorative sewing has resulted in the introduction of all sorts of new materials and threads.

Even with a machine whose only decorative stitch is a zigzag, experimentation with some of the fancy threads can produce very elaborate patterns. A simple yet effective combination is the addition of a line of straight stitch along one side of satin stitch, as shown in figure 21. Vary the effect by choosing complementary or contrasting thread for the trim.

Figure 21. Satin stitch with edging

Many of the vests shown in this book feature intricate and beautiful machine embroidery. (For just two examples, see those on pages 57 and 95.) Embroidery can be used to accent appliquéd pieces, to highlight printed fabrics, or to completely change the look of a fabric, as in the vest on page 55.

A great many decorative threads for machine embroidery have come onto the market over the past several years. Using them may require some adjustments in your sewing techniques and to your machine. When you purchase these threads, ask for the manufacturer's information sheet, and seek the advice of people in the store who have worked with them.

One of the most attractive threads for decorative work is rayon, which gives a nice sheen to the stitching and works well for highlighting. With many machines, the upper tension should be loosened slightly when sewing with rayon.

Metallic threads are fun too. This type of thread sometimes will shear as it passes through the eye of the needle, but there is a needle now available made just for metallic thread, and it solves the problem.

147

Because decorative threads have different thicknesses and different degrees of "slipperiness," you will probably need to alter the machine's suggested or automatic stitch width and length settings to make a decorative stitch look its best. Satin stitches, in particular, are improved by a little fine tuning.

Some of the heavier threads, such as cordonnet, are best used in the bobbin because they are too thick to pass easily through the machine's upper tension mechanism. To use these, bobbin tension has to be adjusted. Bobbin tension adjustment is very critical, so consult the machine instruction book, or ask the dealer how to do this. Experienced sewers who work with these threads keep a second bobbin case adjusted for the heavier threads.

With decorative thread in the bobbin, stitching is done on the wrong side of the fabric. Some decorative stitches look entirely different on the underside; test to see that the results are what you planned.

With almost all embroidery work, a backing of some kind is necessary to prevent the rather dense stitching from puckering the fabric. A light underlining should be adequate with just a little stitching; elaborate stitchery necessitates a stiff backing material. Tear-away backing is a boon with heavy stitching in concentrated areas. It is, however, difficult to remove from an all-over stitch pattern. Aerosol backing works very well with most fabrics. Even plain typing paper can be used behind a stitch pattern, although it will dull the needle in short order. Every combination of machine, fabric, backing, thread, and operator produces different results, and experimentation is the only way to find the best combination for a particular project.

An alternative to using a backing for embroidery stitching is to employ an embroidery hoop. Normally used for hand work, the same wooden hoop can be used to hold your fabric taut while you embroider with your machine. Tighten the fabric in the hoop opposite to the way it's positioned for hand embroidery so that the fabric will lie flat against the machine's sewing surface. Then slip one side of the hoop under the needle of the machine. You may need to remove the presser foot to do this.

Double and triple needles, which work with all machines, can produce some surprisingly intricate and unusual designs. Used with a straight stitch they make a narrow "pintuck" (see the vests on pages 100 and 101). With two or three different thread colors and a decorative stitch, these can almost create their own fabrics! Take care to adjust the stitch width to accommodate the needle's wider swing.

Following a few basic guidelines will contribute a great deal toward the success of any machine embroidery project.

- Allow extra fabric for the piece to be embroidered. Heavy stitching draws up the fabric. Cut the piece approximately 2" (5 cm) larger all around; then trim it to the pattern when the embroidery is finished.

- Always use a backing. The denser you make the stitching, the firmer the backing required. A hoop can also be used, in which case a lighter backing will work.

- Use a needle that is in good condition and appropriate for the thread and fabric.

- Use the correct presser foot for the stitch.

- Sew slowly. With specialty threads, especially, sewing too quickly can distort the stitching, create a tangle, or cause the thread to break.

■ Free-motion embroidery ■

LEARNING THIS TECHNIQUE enables you to stitch in any direction you please, unhampered by the machine's feed mechanism. Practice first with a triple thickness of muslin or scrap cotton to get the feel of the technique.

Fit the sewing machine with a free-hand embroidery foot or a darning foot. If you have neither, then sew without a presser foot. Be *sure* to lower the presser foot bar, even without a presser foot in place, in order to engage the upper thread tension. Set the machine for a straight stitch, and lower the feed dogs. Now sew, moving the fabric at a pace in keeping with the sewing speed. Try to sew and advance the fabric at a moderate speed rather than too slowly. It takes a little practice; don't give up if at first you have a few knots and broken threads!

Once you have the movements coordinated, you'll find all sorts of ways to apply this technique. Straight stitch can produce wonderfully elaborate designs. With satin stitch you can edge appliqués and embroider monograms. Decorative stitches can be worked freehand too, creating some unusual variations.

FABRIC MANIPULATION

THIS ODD HEADING encompasses various methods of changing the texture of a fabric to create drastic changes in its appearance. The vest shown on page 110 is a good sampler of several kinds of fabric manipulation.

These techniques require a great deal of fabric—up to twice the yardage normally needed for a vest. In each case, the altered fabric should be bonded to a lightweight backing, such as light tricot or weft-insertion interfacing. The fabrics are stitched after they're reworked to hold the pleats, tucks, or wrinkles in place. Decorative stitches are interesting to try, and shiny or metallic threads can provide nice contrast.

■ Tucks ■

STRIPED FABRICS beg to be manipulated this way (see pages 58–59). The technique can work beautifully with plaids and checks too.

On the right side of the fabric, fold a tuck and press it. Stitch the tuck parallel to the fold, at a distance appropriate to the pattern. Press the tuck to one side or the other, or to one side *then* the other, to see what happens. Stitch across the tucks to hold them in the pressed positions.

■ Pleats ■

A CRAFTY DEVICE called a fabric pleater (see the photo on page 9) allows large sections of fabric to be pleated neatly and easily. It is made of stiffened canvas, evenly pleated so that fabric can be tucked into its folds and the pleats pressed in place. The fabric should be allowed to cool slightly to set the pleats before removing it from the pleater. The pleated fabric can then be bonded to a backing, and the pleats stitched to secure them.

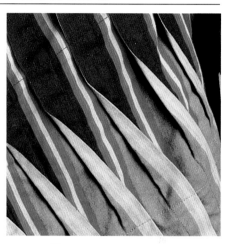

Pleating a striped fabric

Pleaters are available from notions suppliers. They are available in different sizes, and each can produce pleats of varying widths.

■ Crumpling ■

ONE WONDERS how these techniques are first discovered! This one works best on lightweight natural fiber fabrics, especially those that wrinkle easily, such as cotton, linen, and rayon.

Wet the fabric and hold it taut along its length. If the piece is long, have a friend help, or clamp it securely in place. Gather and fold the ends into small pleats, compressing the fabric as tightly as possible. Bind the end with a rubber band or tie it with string. Repeat the process along the length of fabric, tying it at intervals. Holding the fabric taut, twist it along its length until

149

it begins to double back on itself and make a bundle. Tie the bundle securely, and toss it into the dryer until it is dry all the way through. Now untie the fabric and flatten it somewhat. After bonding it to a backing, stitch the wrinkles wherever necessary to keep them in place.

Thanks go to champion fabric wrinkler Becky Brodersen for the specifics of her favorite manipulation procedure. The vests on pages 100 and 101 illustrate how well it works.

HANDWOVEN FABRICS

IF YOU'RE LUCKY ENOUGH to have a piece of handwoven fabric for your vest, remember that a great deal of skill and planning went into its creation, and give it a little special care. Handwovens aren't treated with the same finishing agents used on manufactured fabrics, so they can be quite soft and unstable.

Because of the bias lines in a vest, unstable fabric can cause the garment to stretch out of shape. Soft handwovens should be backed with lightweight fusible interfacing, such as tricot or weft insertion, before the garment is cut. Curved seams should be reinforced with stay tape to prevent their stretching.

PIECING AND PATCHWORK

Many of the vests shown in this book are made with a patchwork fabric created by traditional quilting methods, such as Seminole and crazy quilt. Others vests are pieced, either to add seams in specific places or to elaborate upon fabric features, such as stripes.

To plan a patchwork or pieced design, draw it first on a copy of the pattern to determine a pleasing arrangement of fabrics and lines. These designs essentially create patterned fabrics, and the same guidelines apply. Wide crosswise strips, complex patterning toward the sides of the

garment, or diagonal design lines that slant downward from the center all can add width to the body. Diagonal lines slanting upward from center, darker fabrics used toward the sides of the garment, and piecing that gives the appearance of vertical stripes all have a slimming effect.

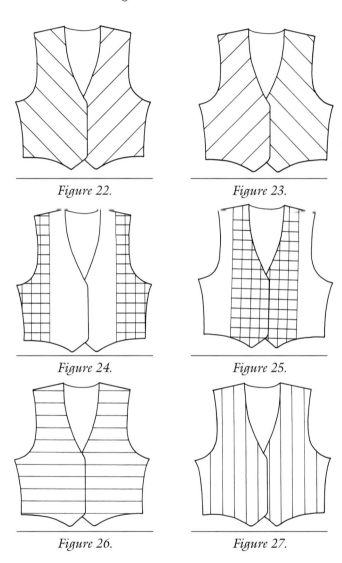

Figure 22.

Figure 23.

Figure 24.

Figure 25.

Figure 26.

Figure 27.

With all pieced and patchwork designs, extra fabric should be allowed around the pattern edges because the seaming required for piecing can condense the fabric somewhat. After assembling the fabric for each vest piece, trim it to the pattern.

■ Pieced designs ■

THERE ARE SEVERAL REASONS for adding seams where none previously existed. Piecing enables you to display a pleasing combination of fabrics and, just for design interest, to rearrange them however you please. By allowing you to cut and offset portions of a single fabric, piecing can create a design feature such as a yoke. Extra seams can have practical benefits too; they provide for the addition of back belts and seamline pockets.

To plan a pieced design, work with a copy of the full-size pattern. Draw lines where you plan to create seams. When you cut your fabric, remember to add a seam allowance to each piece that you create by making a cut. On the pattern, mark an X on each side of each line that you draw to remind you. Mark the lengthwise grain—a line parallel with the center front or center back line—on each piece if you will be cutting from several different fabrics. If you are subdividing the pattern into many pieces, it's a good idea to number them so that you can reassemble them correctly later.

Cut the pieces from the fabric, adding a seam allowance at each edge marked with an X. For a design with many pieces, label them as you did the cut pattern. Then reassemble the cut pattern to use as a construction guide.

■ Patchwork ■

PATCHWORK DESIGNS ADAPT WELL to vests. Even a strip of small pieced fabrics can add considerable design interest to an otherwise simple vest.

Many kinds of patchwork can be applied to vest designs, from old traditional quilting patterns to crazy patchwork and strip quilting. The only "rule" is that the patterns be suitable in scale to the garment.

For traditional patchwork, all-cotton fabrics, light to medium in weight, are the quilter's choice. For crazy patchwork, almost anything goes.

Patchwork garments require a backing to stabilize the pieced fabric. Cotton organdy and muslin work well as a backing for many designs. If the garment will also be quilted, cotton flannel or garment-weight batting will emphasize the stitching.

Patchwork pieces can be cut accurately and quickly with a rotary cutter and mat. In traditional quilting methods, a 1/4" (6-mm) seam allowance is used for piecing. A presser foot is available with one side exactly that width to ensure accuracy, or a piece of tape on the stitch plate can serve as a guide. Press all of the seam allowances to one side.

■ Crazy patch ■

A TECHNIQUE AS OLD AS TIME, this patchwork method involves the random application of patches to a background fabric. Pieces can be stitched in place either by hand or by machine, as

Crazy patch made with a variety of fabrics

with appliqué, and might be decorated with embroidery stitches and metallic or lustrous threads.

A quick, efficient method for sewing crazy patch pieces to a background is the stitch-and-flip technique. Cut a muslin backing slightly larger all around than the pattern. If desired, draw the patch arrangement on the muslin with a black waterproof marking pen so that the lines will show through to the back of the fabric. (This will provide a guide for sewing the patches with decorative threads later.)

Starting at the shoulder, place a patch even with the shoulder edge. Place the next

151

piece upside down on the first, aligning the lower edges of both pieces. Stitch across the lower edge, and flip the second piece downward. Press.

Continue placing patches this way. If an edge of a piece will remain visible after the subsequent patch is sewn, fold under the edge and press before stitching the piece in place.

When patches cover the entire backing, baste around the outer edges. Turn the whole piece over, and stitch along the marked lines with any combination of plain and decorative stitches to secure the patches. Since the bobbin thread will show, use decorative threads in the bobbin if you wish. (See the section on machine embroidery, page 147.) Trim the finished piece to the pattern.

To reduce bulk, crazy patch pieces can also be cut without seam allowances and applied to the vest piece with embroidery stitches to cover the raw edges. A line of liquid fray retardant around the edges of the patches will inhibit raveling, and the stitching will hide any discoloration caused by the liquid.

■ **Seminole, or strip piecing** ■

THIS TECHNIQUE PROVIDES an easy way to create intricate patterns from very small pieces. Simply cut your chosen fabrics into strips, and sew them together. Then cut the resulting pieces perpendicular to the seams, and reassemble them into new patterns. Many elaborate designs are possible; an example is shown in figure 28.

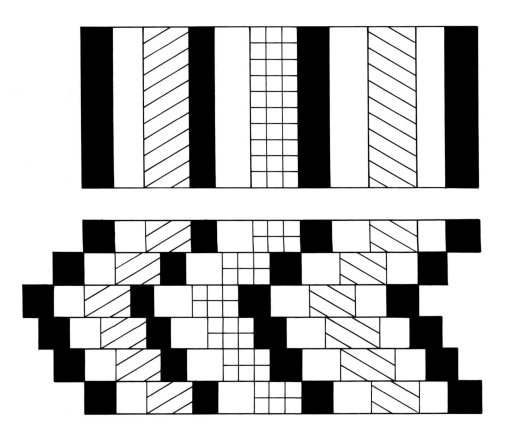

Figure 28. Seminole, or strip piecing

As with other pieced patchwork, accurate cutting and sewing are essential. A rotary cutter and mat are helpful for precise cutting, and a quilter's presser foot keeps the seams exact.

POCKETS

THE TERM "VEST POCKET" has come to describe something small that's tucked into a minimal amount of space. There isn't sufficient room on the front of a vest for full-scale pockets, so the designers have engineered several clever vest-pocket ideas.

In the following instructions, the seam allowances are 5/8" (1.6 cm) except where noted.

■ Add-on pocket ■

THE VEST ON PAGE 36 sports pockets that are quite roomy, yet they're in proportion to the garment. For added interest, the pockets are lined with the same print fabric that lines the vest.

Make a pattern for the pocket by tracing across the "lengthen/shorten" line and around the front and lower edges of the front pattern piece. Add a seam allowance across the upper edge of the pocket, where the cut was made. Now cut two pieces (a left and a right) from the vest fabric and two from the lining.

With right sides together, sew each pocket to its lining across the upper edge. Turn, press, and topstitch.

Machine baste the pocket to the vest front along the unfinished edges, and construct the vest in the standard way. A line of vertical stitching about halfway across makes two pockets of each one, and prevents sagging.

■ Visible in-seam pocket ■

ON EACH SIDE OF THE VEST on page 106, a piecing seam allows for an interesting arrangement of fabrics and provides seams to tuck in two very small pockets, perhaps just large enough for an antique pocket watch or two theater tickets.

Draw cutting lines across the vest in the chosen locations. Then cut the fabrics for the pieces, remembering to add seam allowances where the cuts were made. Cut the rest of the fabrics for the vest front.

Both finished pockets are only 1-1/2" (3.8 cm) deep; the upper pocket is 3" (7.6 cm) wide; the lower one is 5" (12.7 cm) wide. Draw patterns for these pieces, adding seam allowances on all sides. Then cut one of each from the vest fabric and from the lining fabric. Stitch each pocket to its lining at the sides and upper edge. Then trim the seams, turn the pockets right side out, and press. Topstitch across the upper edge if desired.

Placing the raw edges together, baste each pocket to the seam allowance of the appropriate vest piece, and stitch the seam. After pressing the pockets upward, topstitch them to the vest at the sides.

■ Invisible in-seam pocket ■

THIS POCKET ALSO REQUIRES a horizontal piecing seam in the front of the vest. On the vest shown on page 116, the pocket is at the lower left, but it could be placed on the upper part of the vest instead.

Draw a cutting line across the vest front pattern piece at the desired pocket location. Cut the vest pieces, adding 3/4" (about 2 cm) seam allowances at the piecing seamline. Stitch the vest sections together along the piecing seam, leaving the seam open where the pocket will be. Press the seams open. Topstitch above and below the pocket opening.

Cut two pieces of lining fabric, 1-1/4" (3.2 cm) wider than the pocket opening, and about 1" (2.5 cm) longer than the desired finished pocket length (length isn't critical at this point). With right sides together, pin one lining section to each pocket opening seam allowance, centering the lining over the pocket opening. Stitch 1/4" (6 mm) from the edge. Press the seams toward the lining, and stitch each seam allowance to the lining. Fold the upper pocket section downward, aligning it along the sides with the lower pocket lining. Now mark the seamline across the bottom at the desired point. Stitch the sides and bottom. On the outside, stitch across each end of the pocket opening for reinforcement.

To include a buttonhole tab with your pocket, cut a lengthwise strip of fabric 1-1/2" (3.8 cm) wide and 4" (10.2 cm) long. With wrong sides together, press the strip in half along its length. Fold the raw edges 1/4" (6 mm) to the inside; press. Edgestitch the folded edges together, and edgestitch the opposite long edge. After folding the strip in half, flatten the fold to form a point (see figure 29). Stitch across the base

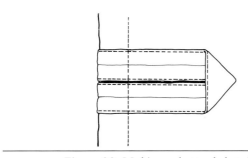

Figure 29. Making a buttonhole tab

of the point to secure it. Baste the tab ends side by side to the seam allowance of the upper pocket opening, centered in the opening and with tab ends even with the edge of the seam allowance. Position the upper pocket lining section, and stitch as described above. Sew a button to the outer pocket beneath the tab.

■ Lined patch pocket ■

THIS TYPE OF POCKET can be seen on the vest on page 46. Before sewing the pocket to the vest, the designer added ribbon and fringe trim to the pocket's upper edge. Your version can be decorated to suit your own design, or it can be left plain. A pocket template, which you can purchase from a notions supplier or make from a piece of cardboard, produces evenly rounded lower corners.

For the outer pocket, cut the fabric 2-1/4" (5.7 cm) longer and 1-1/4" (3.2 cm) wider than the desired finished pocket size. Cut the lining fabric the same width and about 2" (5 cm) shorter. Trim 1/16" (1.5 mm) from the sides and lower edge of the lining.

With right sides together, stitch the pocket to the lining along the upper edge, leaving about 2" (5 cm) open at the center of the seam for turning. (See figure 30.) Press the seam allowances toward the lining.

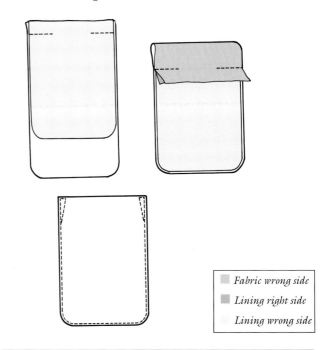

Fabric wrong side
Lining right side
Lining wrong side

Figure 30. Lined patch pocket

Still on the wrong side, pull the lining fabric down to make a fold across the outer fabric about 1" (2.5 cm) above the seamline, aligning the sides and lower edges of both pocket pieces. Stitch the sides and lower edge, stretching the lining to fit. Now trim the seams, and turn the pocket right side out. Press so that the outer fabric extends slightly beyond the lining. Topstitch or add trimming to the upper edge, if desired. Finally, pin the pocket to the vest, and stitch it in place close to the edges, stitching a triangle at the upper edges for security.

QUILTING

A simple design enhanced with quilting

QUILTING IS SIMPLY a matter of backing a fabric with a second fabric that has some thickness, then stitching through both layers to create a design with a dimensional quality. Quilting can be used to outline a motif or highlight other design lines of the fabric. On a plain fabric, it can create patterns that are subtle or dramatic, depending upon the thread and stitches used. Quilting can be done with decorative stitches, along with decorative threads, or with a thread that contrasts with the color of the fabric. A look at the photos on pages 55, 61, 68, 71, and 75 will give you an idea of the great variety of ways in which quilting can be used.

Many of the special quilting techniques used by the designers are included with the descriptions of their vests. The suggestions that follow apply to quilted garments in general.

A quilted garment is thicker, and quilting produces a firm fabric without drape. It might be a good idea to make the vest slightly smaller than normal so that it doesn't stand out from the body. Since quilted fabric produces very bulky seams, the vest should be constructed according to the alternate method described on page 31, and the edges bound. Many sewing machines will not produce a good buttonhole in such thick fabric. Try one of the alternatives discussed on pages 139–42.

Allow an extra 2" or so (about 5 cm) around the edges of the pattern pieces when cutting, as quilting will condense the fabric. After quilting each piece, recut it to the pattern.

The quilter's fabric of choice is 100 percent cotton. Blends of polyester and cotton tend to stretch and pucker along the stitching lines. Some silks, such as medium-weight crepe and noil, also adapt well to quilting. Very lightweight wool, challis, for example, works too.

For backing, cotton flannel is an excellent choice. Garment-weight polyester batting, available from quilting suppliers, is another good bet.

Before starting a quilting project, please also read the section on embroidery, beginning on page 146. Many of the procedures and materials are the same for both techniques.

To stitch the quilting lines, you may need to loosen the presser foot pressure slightly if your machine allows this adjustment. Otherwise, use a presser foot that doesn't press so tightly against the fabric, such as the clear appliqué foot, or the walking or even-feed foot.

155

■ Trapunto ■

TRAPUNTO IS A QUILTING TECHNIQUE that involves stitching around a pattern motif in the fabric, or stitching a design onto the fabric, then stuffing the stitched area to give it dimension. The trapunto technique is used in the vest on page 54 to highlight the coyotes under the sequined moon.

For trapunto quilting, underline the vest pieces with light- to medium-weight cotton, such as lawn or muslin. Outline a motif or two by stitching through both layers, or stitch a pattern of your own design. On the back, carefully cut a slit behind each stitched area, cutting through just the underlining. Stuff the areas with small pieces of fleece or fiberfill; then stitch the cut closed.

Dylan Babb, age 10, is an honor student as well as a dancer and a beginning vest maker. She lives in Asheville, North Carolina.

Joyce Baldwin, a lifelong seamstress and clothing designer, teaches textile and tailoring courses at Western Carolina University in Cullowhee, North Carolina.

Jimmie Benedict, of Reno, Nevada, is a professional designer who specializes in the creation of distinctive wearable art.

Becky Brodersen especially enjoys experimenting with fabric manipulation techniques. She is a professional weaver and vest maker in Nashville, Tennessee.

Betty Carlson, of Bryson City, North Carolina, took early retirement from a career in medical technology to pursue her passion for weaving.

Cathy Carlson is a professional needlework designer, specializing in traditional Norwegian stitchery. She lives in Asheville, North Carolina.

Pam Cauble, an enthusiastic quilter, hat maker, and Spanish teacher, lives in Asheville, North Carolina.

Charlie Covington's artistic pursuits range from computer graphics to wearable sculpture. He lives in Asheville, North Carolina.

Beverly Dawson and *Lynda Sanders* produce one-of-a-kind clothing and accessories through their business, Appliquétions by Design, located in Chapel Hill, North Carolina.

Allison Dennis, of Russellville, Kentucky, creates and sells unique clothing made from her own handwoven fabrics.

Leslie Dierks, this book's editor, was overtaken by vest-making fever and couldn't resist making one of her own.

Nancy Fleming is an Asheville, North Carolina, metalsmith who happened upon a vest while exploring unconventional ways to use found materials.

Suzanne Gernandt loves textiles in every form. She lives in Asheville, North Carolina, and devotes all her spare time to weaving.

Nancy Granner teaches weaving and quilting from a home base in Nashville, Tennessee. She is known for her crazy quilt Christmas ornaments—one of which has decorated the White House tree.

Niessa Bauder Guaracha's specialty is custom-designed embroidered clothing. She lives in Hollister, California.

Beth Hill, of Asheville, North Carolina, spends most of her time creating with fabric. Her specialty (vests notwithstanding) is superbly crafted bears.

157

Rachel Hill, shortly after completing her decorated vest, was named "Artist of the Month" in her second grade class. She lives in Norristown, Pennsylvania.

Dana Irwin, in addition to being the art director for this book, is a painter and a resolute collector of interesting textiles—and any other raw materials that exhibit great potential.

Elma Johnson is an artist with diverse talents. She works in ceramics, brick, glass, paper, and textiles, and she teaches most of these skills at the University of North Carolina, Asheville.

Susan Kinney began an interior design career in her native Hawaii and expanded her interests to include jewelry design and fabric experimentation when she relocated to Asheville.

Suzanne Koppi has sewn professionally for many years. With her present career in special education, sewing provides a relaxing creative outlet. She lives in Asheville, North Carolina.

Dale Liles is a professional felt maker in Knoxville, Tennessee. She creates garments from fleece that she colors with natural dyes and trims with handspun yarns. She travels extensively to teach felt making and to demonstrate the processing of her own home-grown flax.

Liz Lima, of Asheville, North Carolina, is a professional dressmaker who teaches classes in a variety of creative sewing techniques.

Lori Kerr designs fabric jewelry and textile art pieces as well as vests, but she most enjoys sharing her skills through teaching. She lives in Durham, North Carolina.

Sherry Masters first learned to sew from her two grandmothers. Working in the retail end of the crafts business and teaching sewing classes have inspired her interest in creative sewing and garment design. She lives in Asheville, North Carolina.

Peggy McClure is a multi-talented sewer who is especially fond of designing Victorian heirloom clothing. She teaches classes in Asheville, North Carolina, in the creation of wearable art.

Pat Moore received formal design training through a degree in fine arts and has applied it to almost every form of needlework. She particularly enjoys adding fine handwork to pieces from her collection of old textiles. She owns an heirloom sewing shop, Mimi's Fabrications, in Waynesville, North Carolina.

Becky Orr works with the Southern Highland Handicraft Guild in Asheville, North Carolina. Two children leave her little free time—and it all goes to sewing and quilting.

Mary Parker pursues a career in public sector finance in order to indulge her passion for fabric. She lives in Asheville, North Carolina with five well-fed cats and "the world's best husband."

Jean Wall Penland is a professional artist—and the proud holder of a new M.F.A. degree—who paints on both canvas and silk. She is an inspiring teacher of silk-painting techniques, conducting classes through an Asheville, North Carolina, craft supply store.

Judith Robertson, of Asheville, North Carolina, sews up almost as much fabric as she acquires—a monumental accomplishment!—and still finds time for gardening, bird watching, music, and earning a living.

Bird Ross is a professional fiber artist in Madison, Wisconsin. She enjoys experimenting with fabrics and using them in unconventional ways.

Maggie Rotman learned her needlework skills during her school days in England. She currently lives in Asheville, North Carolina, where she designs and creates clothing.

Laura Sims marbles fabric professionally in Asheville, North Carolina. Her company, Indigo Stone, produces distinctive marbled clothing and jewelry. Perhaps because the process is a messy one, her workshops are especially popular with children!

Liz Spear combines her weaving and sewing skills to create distinctive handmade garments for small shops and galleries. She lives in Waynesville, North Carolina.

Robbie Spivey, of Asheville and Blowing Rock, North Carolina, considers needlework the highest form of expression, and creates garments as a means of preserving memories, history, and dreams. She has spent upwards of 500 hours on a single vest.

Karen James Swing is a professional vest maker in Boone, North Carolina. Her unique vests often feature intricate quilting patterns on hand-dyed fabrics.

Pat Taylor is a self-taught professional fiber artist and quilt maker in Winston-Salem, North Carolina. She specializes in one-of-a-kind quilted garments made of hand-dyed and dye-painted natural fiber fabrics.

Jennifer Thomas, of Asheville, North Carolina, applies her artistic talents to a range of materials from clay to fiber, and she spends much of her time teaching her skills to her two young daughters.

158

ACKNOWLEDGMENTS

Heartfelt thanks to all of the designers for their creative spirit, their hard work, and their helpful suggestions. And thanks to the special people in *their* lives for whom many of these vests were made and who, if somewhat reluctantly, parted with their treasures long enough for us to photograph them.

A very special note of thanks to talented fiber artist Pat Scheible. Her six vests—created just for this book—were lost in transit.

Sincere thanks to all who assisted with the photography: Robin Cape and Ivo Ballentine at Preservation Hall, Linda Constable at Sluder Furniture, Craig Culbertson and Otto Hauser at Stuf Antiques, Lorin Knouse at Southerlands, Steve Kuell at Weststar Photographic, Alan Levy at Gentlemen's Gallery, the Masterpiece Jewelers staff, Ronnie Myers at Magnolia Beauregard's Antiques, Rob Pulleyn, and Amy Texido, all of Asheville, North Carolina.

Special thanks to Ronnie Myers and Paul Rifkin for their generous loan of historic vests.

And thanks to our models, all "regular folks" who took time out of their day to don some fabulous vests for the camera: Dylan Babb, Betty Clark, Carol Covington, Charlie Covington, Anna Katherine Easterby, Jackie Easterby, Sam Easterby, Michael Faulkner, Jenny Gladding, Karen Ives, Beverly Jennings, Kathryn Koppi, Chris Lenderman, Jean McQueen, Deborah Morgenthal, Mathew O'Connell, Connie Schrader, Chuck Spearman, Amy Texido, and Bob Volmerhausen.

INDEX